ARANDORA CROSSING

by david shaw

based on a story by Cinzia Valente

Best Wishes & lots of love David.

Arandora Crossing

written and illustrated by David Shaw

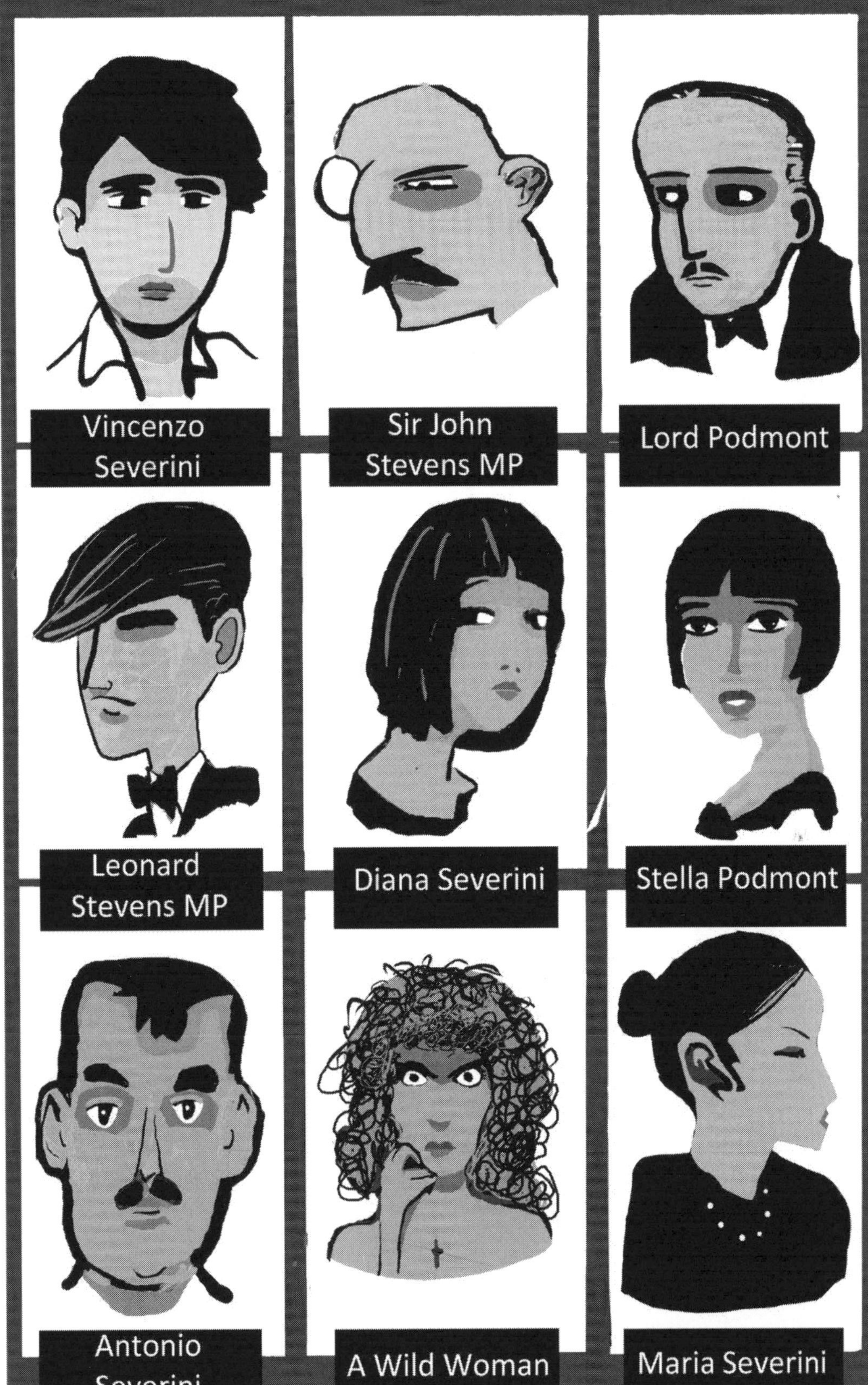
Vincenzo Severini
Sir John Stevens MP
Lord Podmont
Leonard Stevens MP
Diana Severini
Stella Podmont
Antonio Severini
A Wild Woman
Maria Severini

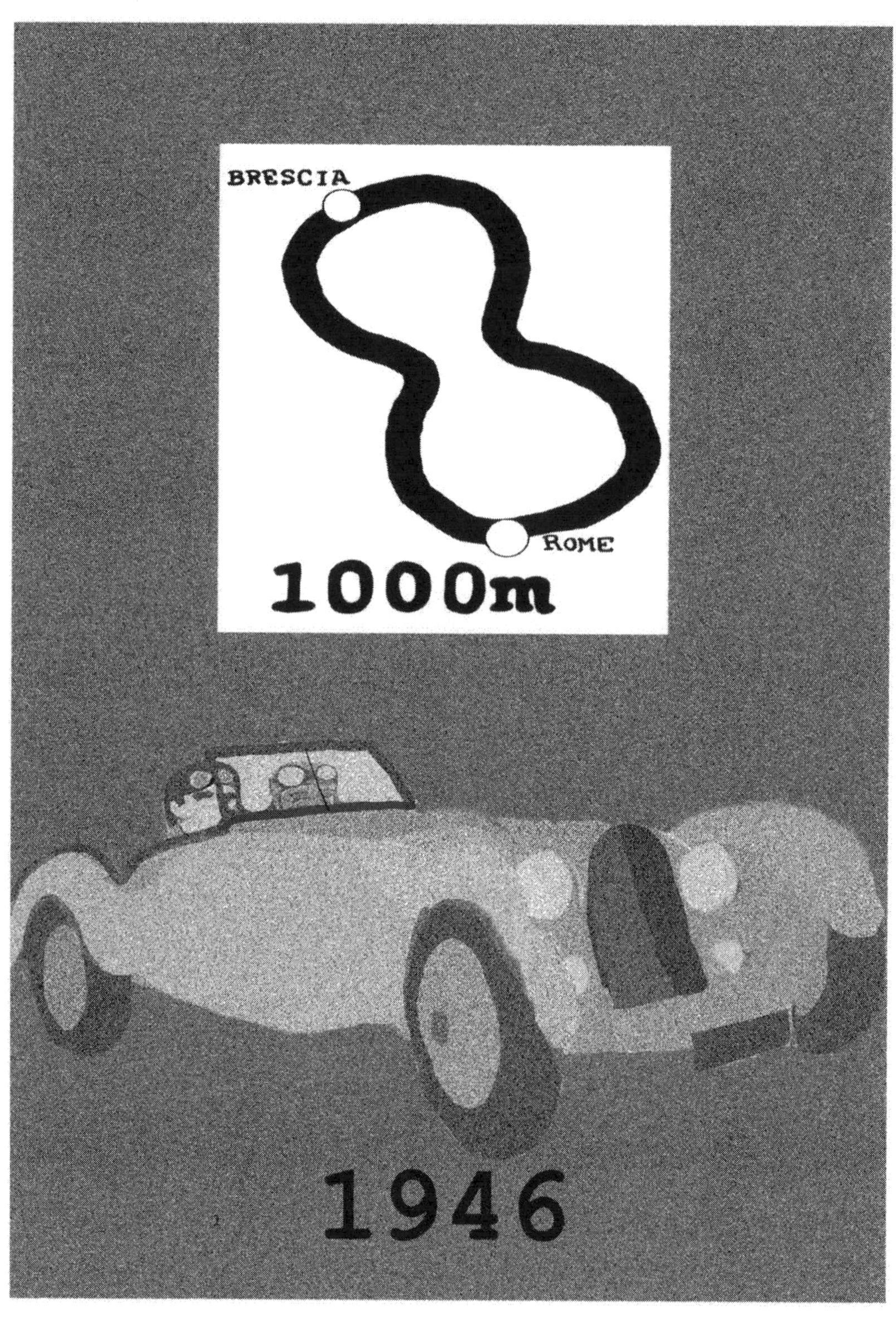

It is little over a year since the end of the war in Europe
and its greatest road race is about to begin.
For a moment one might be forgiven
for forgetting that such carnage ever happened.

Relax Podmont! Five hundred miles south and the same again north. Tell me when to break and when to accelerate. That's all.
BRESCIA
VEROÑA
VICENZA
PADUA
PARMA
BOLOGNA
RAVENNA
FLORENCE
ANCONA
SIENA
VITERBO
PESCARA
ROME
Cheer up! It's not exactly the stations of the cross.
I'm hoping to avoid the same painful outcome.
Just focus on resurrection and eternal life.

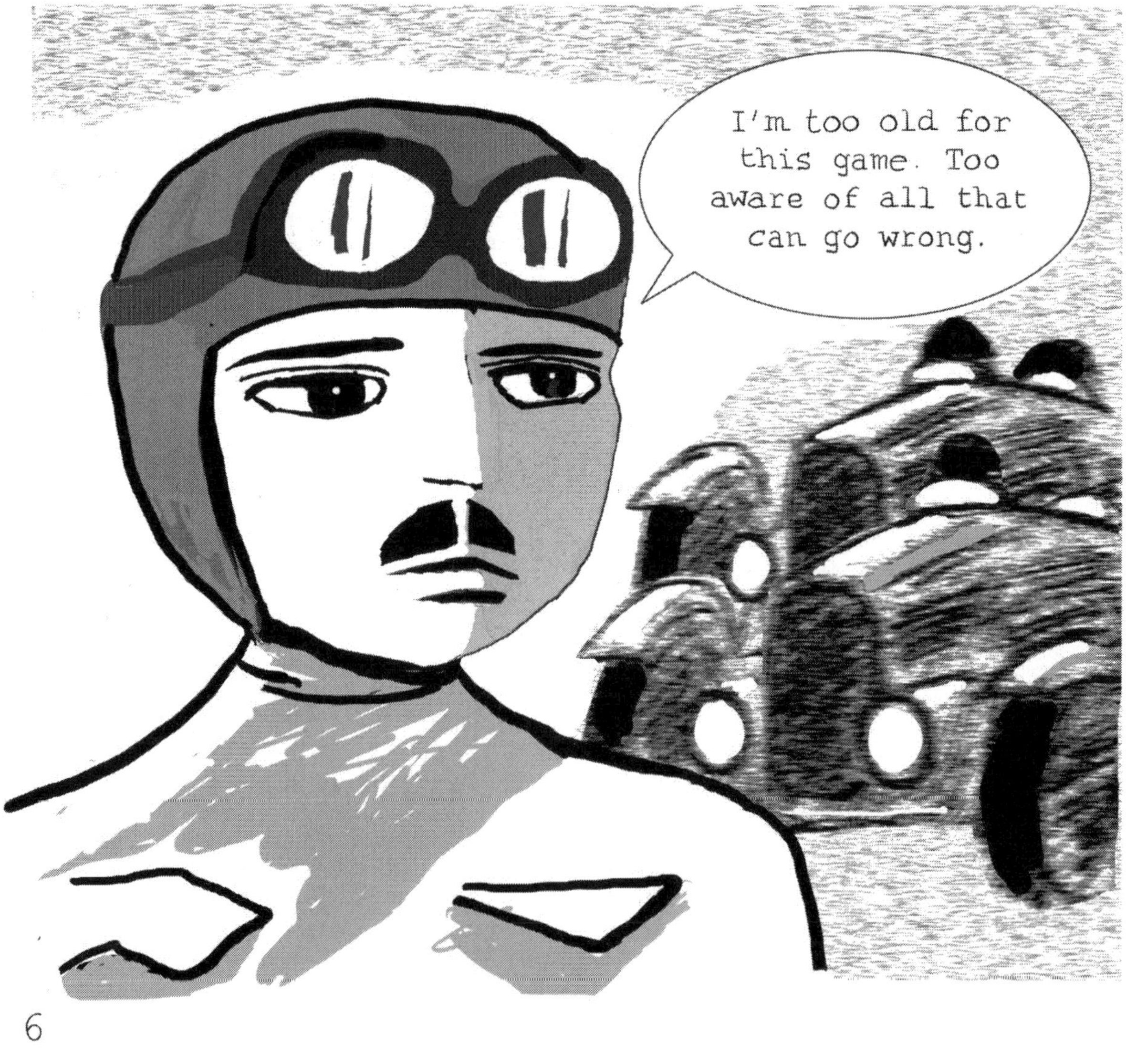

I'm too old for this game. Too aware of all that can go wrong.

Just have faith.

You've got the cross?

Do you suppose that mother or Stella would let me race without it? There's no guarantee for you.

It's not me I worry about.

Last time I was here I drove and your father sat with the map.
And Poppa would have told you there's just a minute to go.

And we're off!

This is essentially that great man's car.
Just let us focus on winning the race.

Vincenzo, you know what I wish for.

Even you can't turn the clock back.

For now just concentrate on the present dangerous corners.

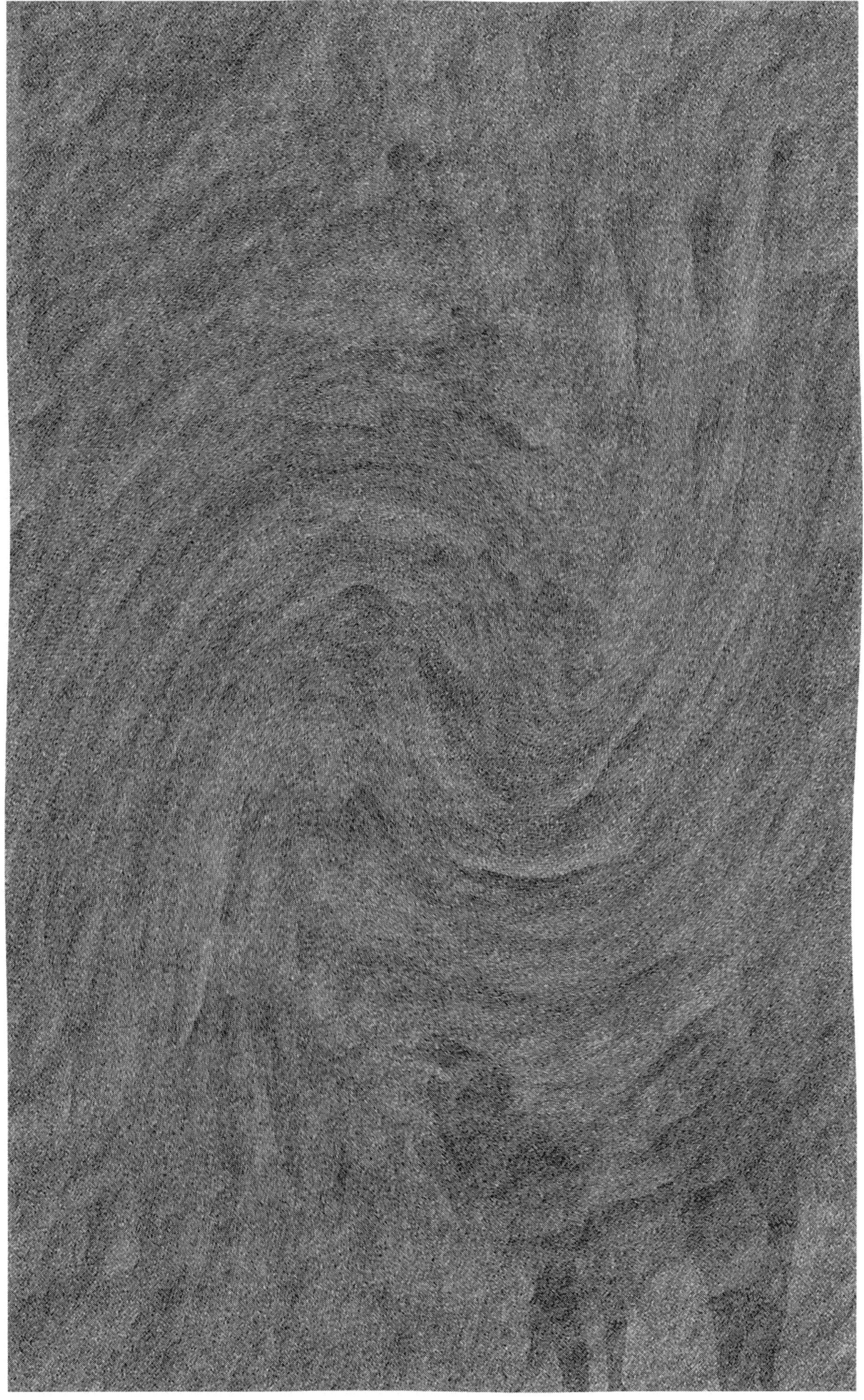

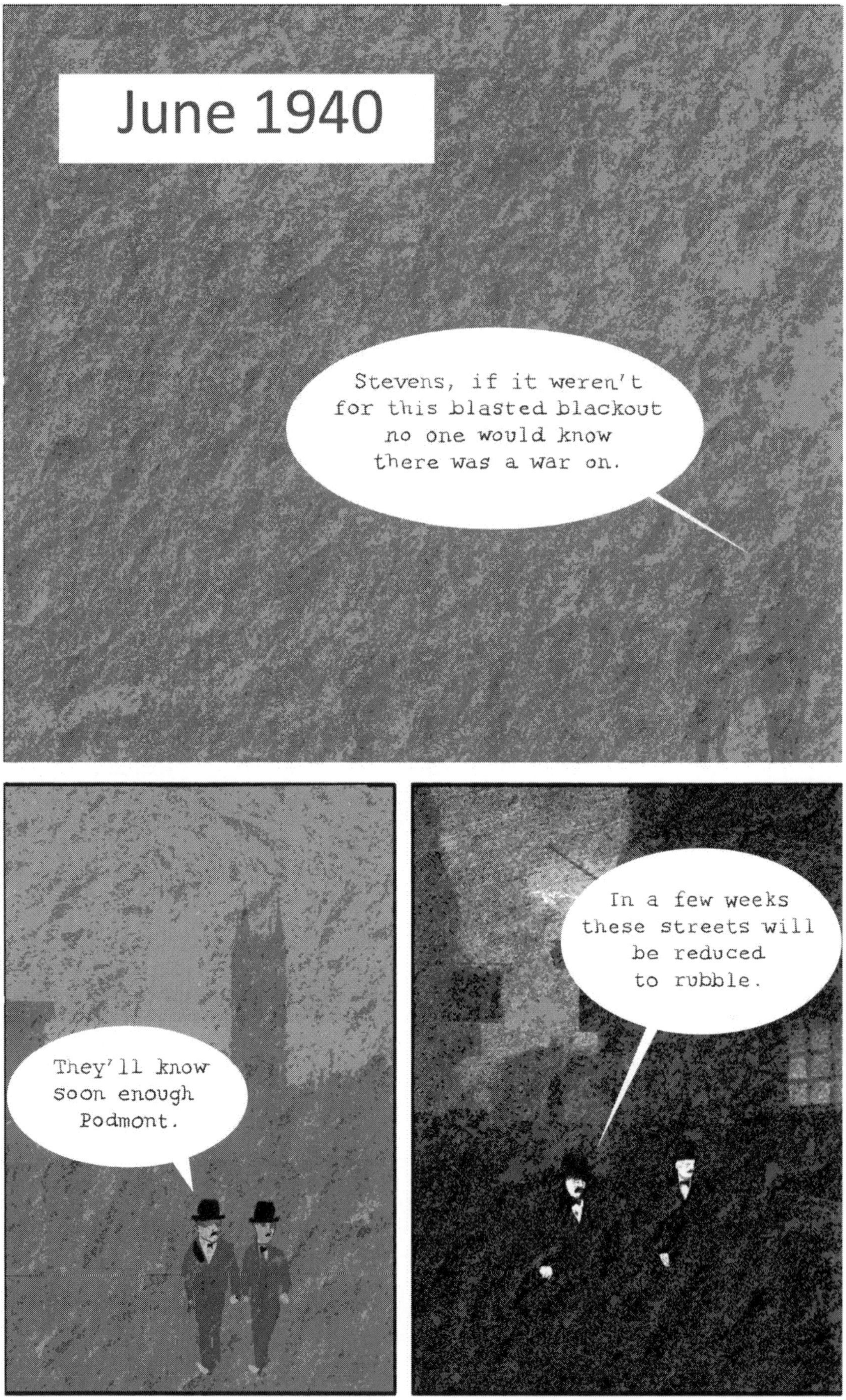

June 1940

Stevens, if it weren't for this blasted blackout no one would know there was a war on.

The world will have
changed for ever.

Isn't this all
a bit cloak
and dagger?

We could be hanged
for just contemplating
what we're doing.

The little foreign
chap is in
the basement.

This is to be
gestapo
head quarters.
Don't even
joke!

They have a long list
containing some
interesting names.
It'll be worse
if Winston
carries on.

Meet Signore Salvatori
actor
and orator.
He was touring
the halls when
Musso declared war.

He helped with
Il Duce's presentation
skills and was loaned
to Hitler and now
he's been loaned
to us.

His troupe has a following in northern resorts.
But with the fall of France and Italy lining up against us....
How quickly laughter turned to howls of rage.
Ultimately they were only saved from lynching by the intervention of the constabulary.

It's to be hoped that you might address your people more effectively.
I am not a bombast!

Podmont, you sound like a vicar.

Leave this to us constable we're going to do some in depth interrogation.

Podmont, look, listen and learn from a master.

ALL' ARMI
ALL' ARMI
ALL' ARMI!
FORTE!
FORTE!
FORTE!
SIAM FASCISTI!

ALL' ARMI!
LA PATRIA NOSTRA!

That's a language everyone understands.
I'm not flamboyant. I'm only at ease in crash helmet and goggles.

You're the man who won't surrender the steering wheel even in practice.
I have a morbid fear of losing control.

This is your time Podmont! Time to take control of a nation!
Get up here with us and feel the power.

I'm a technician. A back room boy.

CANNON TO THE RIGHT! CANNON TO THE LEFT! SOMEONE HAD BLUNDERED!

FORZA! FORZA!
INTO THE VALLEY OF DEATH RODE THE SIX HUNDRED.

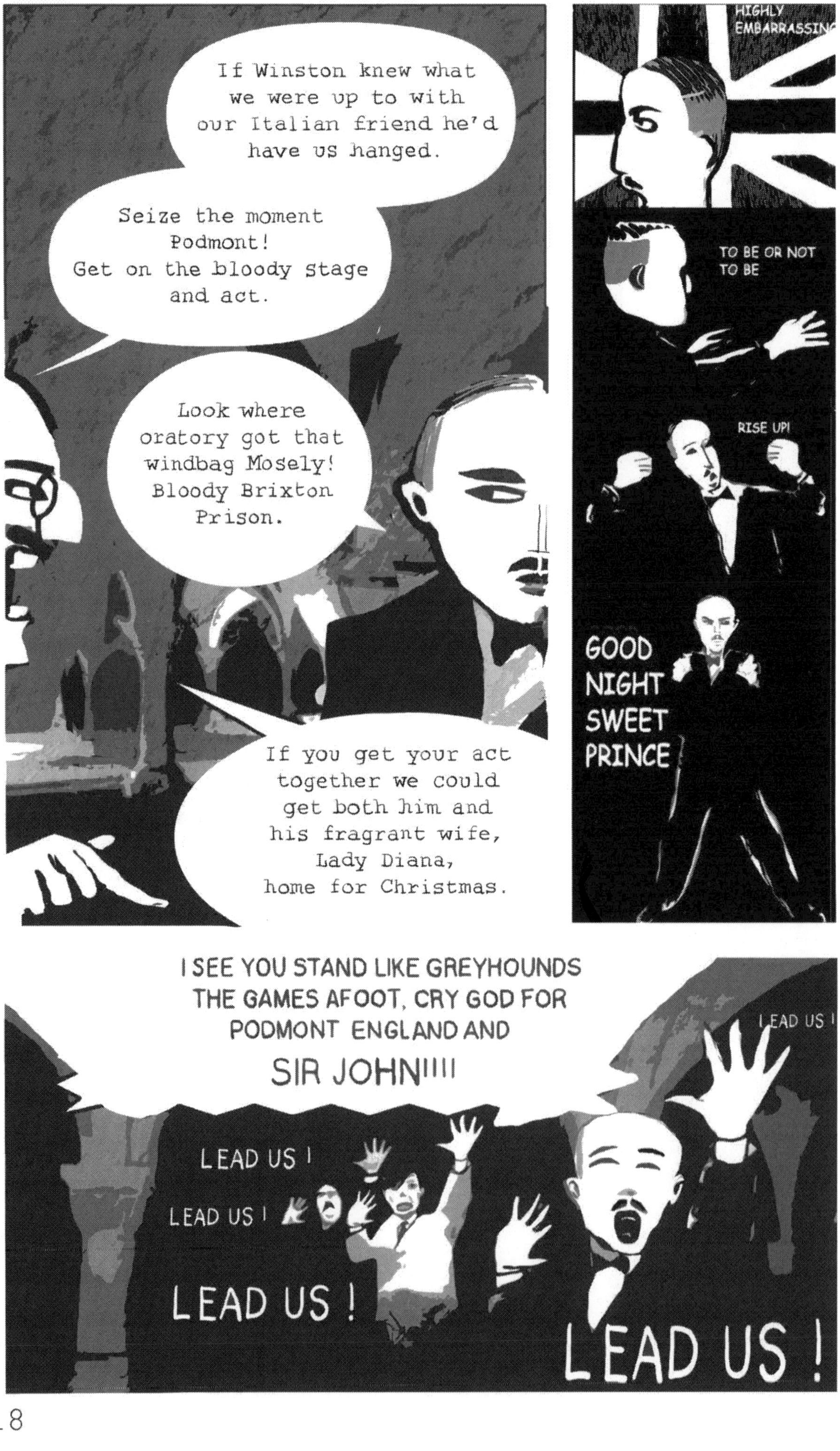

If Winston knew what we were up to with our Italian friend he'd have us hanged.

Seize the moment Podmont! Get on the bloody stage and act.

Look where oratory got that windbag Mosely! Bloody Brixton Prison.

If you get your act together we could get both him and his fragrant wife, Lady Diana, home for Christmas.

HIGHLY EMBARRASSIN

TO BE OR NOT TO BE

RISE UP!

GOOD NIGHT SWEET PRINCE

Heil Podmont!
The whole nation shall chant your name.
And I can hear the creaking of the gallows' floor.

We must resist pandering to the volatile mob!
The powdered aristocrat's fear of the great unwashed!

Don't worry old boy! In six months the mob will be on the Russian front.
Aren't we supposed to be anti-war?
Only those we lose.

PODMONT
PODMONT

June 27th 1940
The skies over
the village of
Podmont in the
county of Kent
just south of London

The activity
in the skies
is intense.

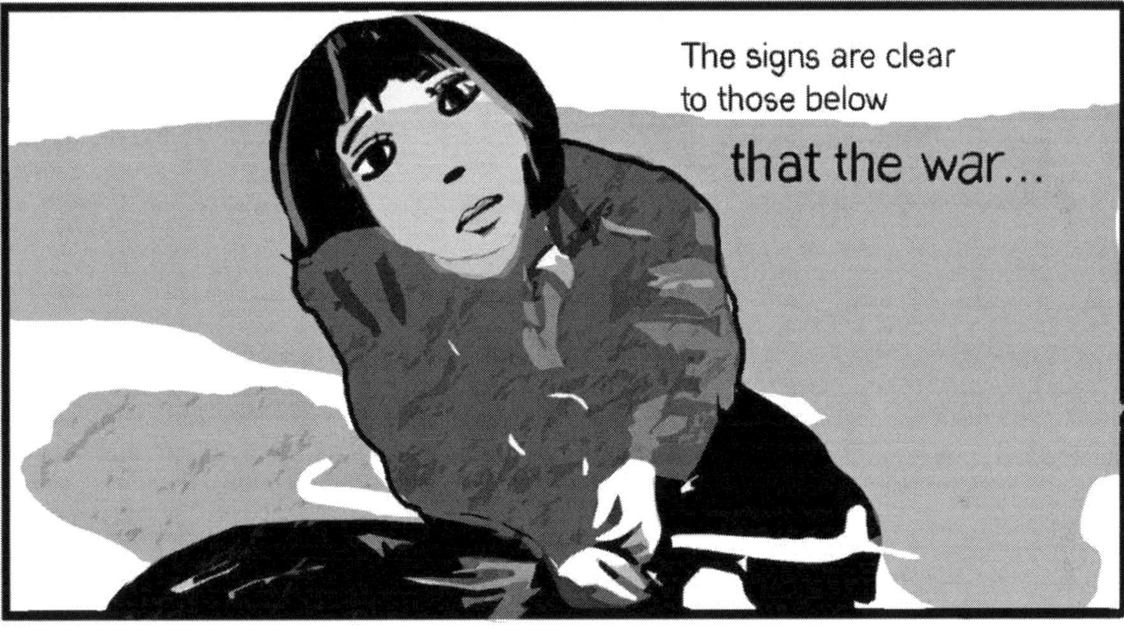
The signs are clear
to those below
that the war...

is shifting closer
to home

Not only
in the skies...

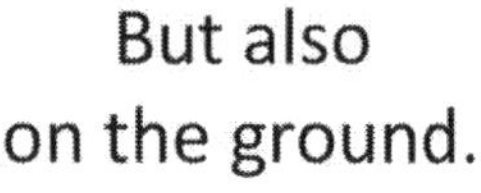

But also
on the ground.

The tension
could be felt everywhere.

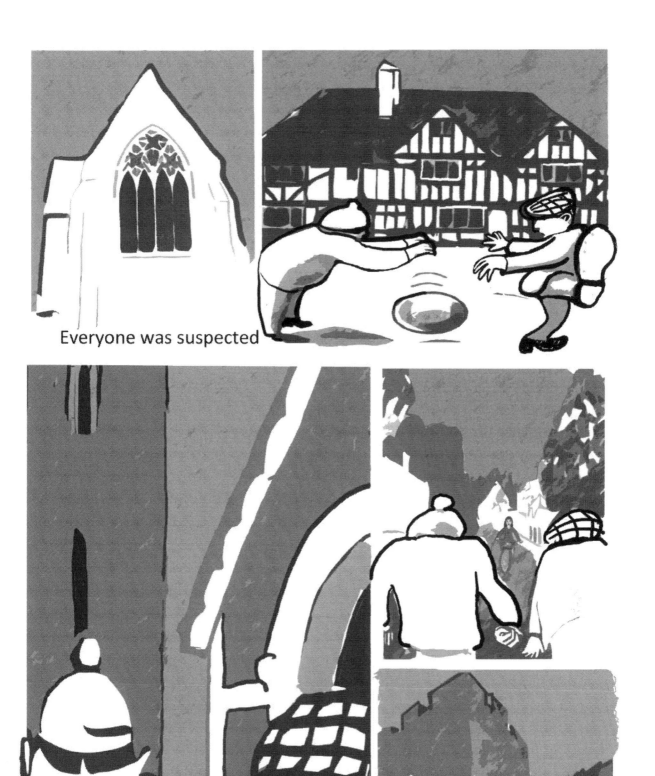

Everyone was suspected

Many were on the look-out for signs of enemy activity.

Enter Diana Severini
Beloved daughter of Maria and Antonio.
Both parents are loyal employees and friends of the Podmont family.
She has lived all her life in England but suddenly she is Italian again.
We're on alien watch. What's in the basket?
O dear! I've left my secret radio at home.
For my needlework class. Why don't you come? You could help the war effort.

We house you,
we educate you,
we give you
the best jobs....

Treat you nicely.
Then, what
do you do?

GET IN WITH
HITLER!

this here bike is requisitioned.

For the defence
of our great nation!

Against you and your kind!

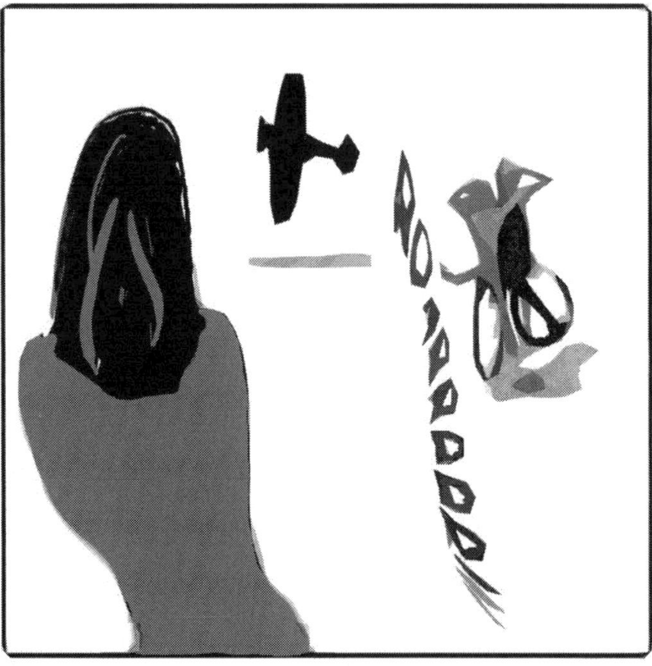

BRMMMMM

ROARRRRR

Enter Lady Stella Podmont

Only and beloved
daughter of
Lord Podmont

Screech!

Diana darling! Hop in!

You mustn't be upset. Daddy will deal with those two oiks.

It's not just them though. Is it?
Isn't it though? Surely all decent people know who our real enemies are?

FAST!
She's brilliant. All down to Antonio and Vincenzo.
You have no worries. There is no way daddy would ever let them go.
He is so honoured to have them on his race team.
When you hadn't been seeing Vincenzo I assumed it was on your daddy's orders.
We're just lying low. Till the clouds clear.

I assumed you had
fallen out of love.

We're closer
than ever.
It's as
romantic
as some
fairy tale.

Star crossed lovers
with a secret passion.
That's us.

Diana there
is something
you could do.
Of course..
but....

I do
hope for
a happy
ending.

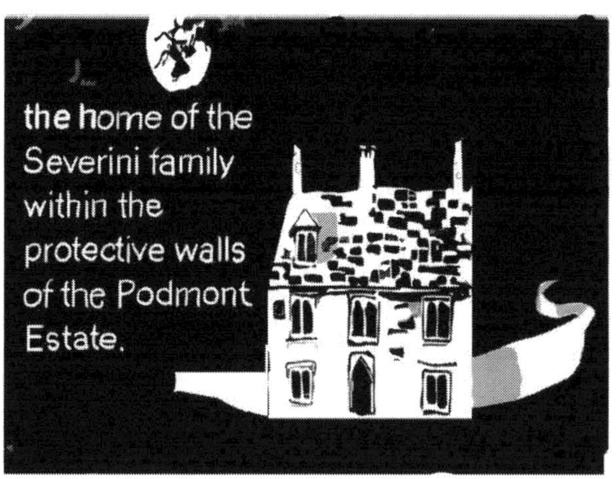
the home of the
Severini family
within the
protective walls
of the Podmont
Estate.

Churchill wants all
Italians detained.

And the most dangerous
are to be deported pronto.

It's still safer
for us here than
with the fascists.

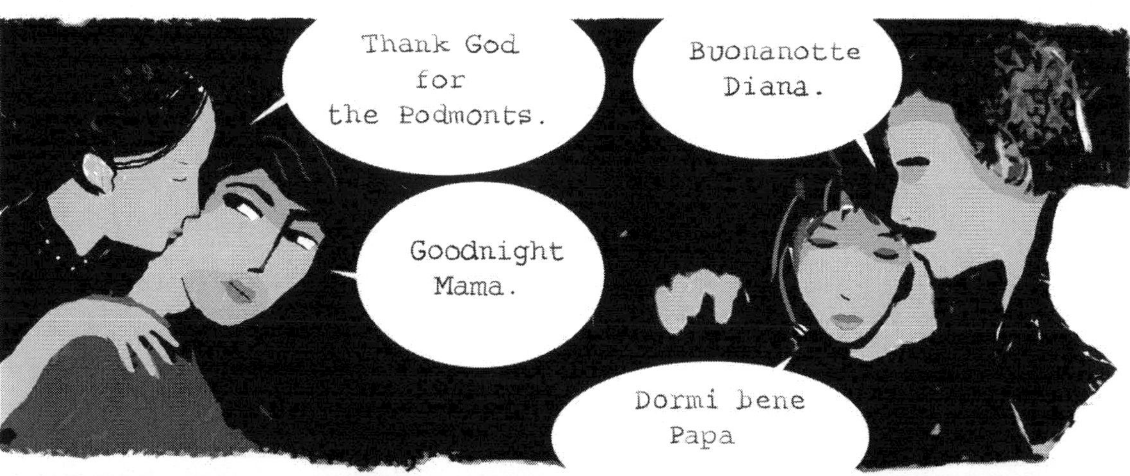
Thank God
for
the Podmonts.
Goodnight
Mama.
Buonanotte
Diana.
Dormi bene
Papa

Vincenzo,
there are
people
who have it
in for us.

Apparently Lord Podmont is going to lead a government of appeasers.
The secret is not to panic.

There's an item here about parachuting nuns.
COLLIR THE LOT

Diana newspapers print garbage. And always will.
I can smell Stella's perfume.

I saw her today

Did she send something for me?

A note. On scented paper.

Did you read it?
Of course. It's beautiful.

I wonder if I could be shot for passing secrets to the enemy?

Romance wouldn't be romantic if it wasn't dangerous.

10

10
DOWNING
STREET
June 28th
1940
The war goes badly.
The press smell
political blood.
Sir John and his son
Leonard emerge.
Has Winston
resigned yet?
Do we
fight on?
Who do
you think
gave
me this
cigar?
It is thought that
Herr Hitler would prefer
Lord Podmont to lead
the country.
Will the king
be going to
Canada?
Time's up chaps.
There's still a
war to run.

Those are a pair
of slippery customers.

Where to today
Mr Private Secretary?
Inspect river
defences then
lunch with
Podmont.

We will use the time to fill
you in on the latest
developments
young Leonard.
TRAITORS
IN
OUR
MIDST

Everyone expects
you to act when
the first bomb
drops on the city.
How were things
today in the house
and war cabinet?

No one sane thinks we can win and consequently our support grows.

Are you convinced that Podmont is ready to wield so much power?
Leonard the situation is most grave. Civilian casualties may be in the millions.

German planes will fill these skies.
Their noise will cause terror!

The mob will be rioting on the streets.
A strong leader will emerge.

Podmont will be that leader.

You paint a depressing picture.
but,alas, accurate.
If all is so clear why wait?
Timing is everything. Too early and we will be branded as spineless.
Too late and German victory is absolute.
Some more blood must be spilt.
If only to satisfy national pride.

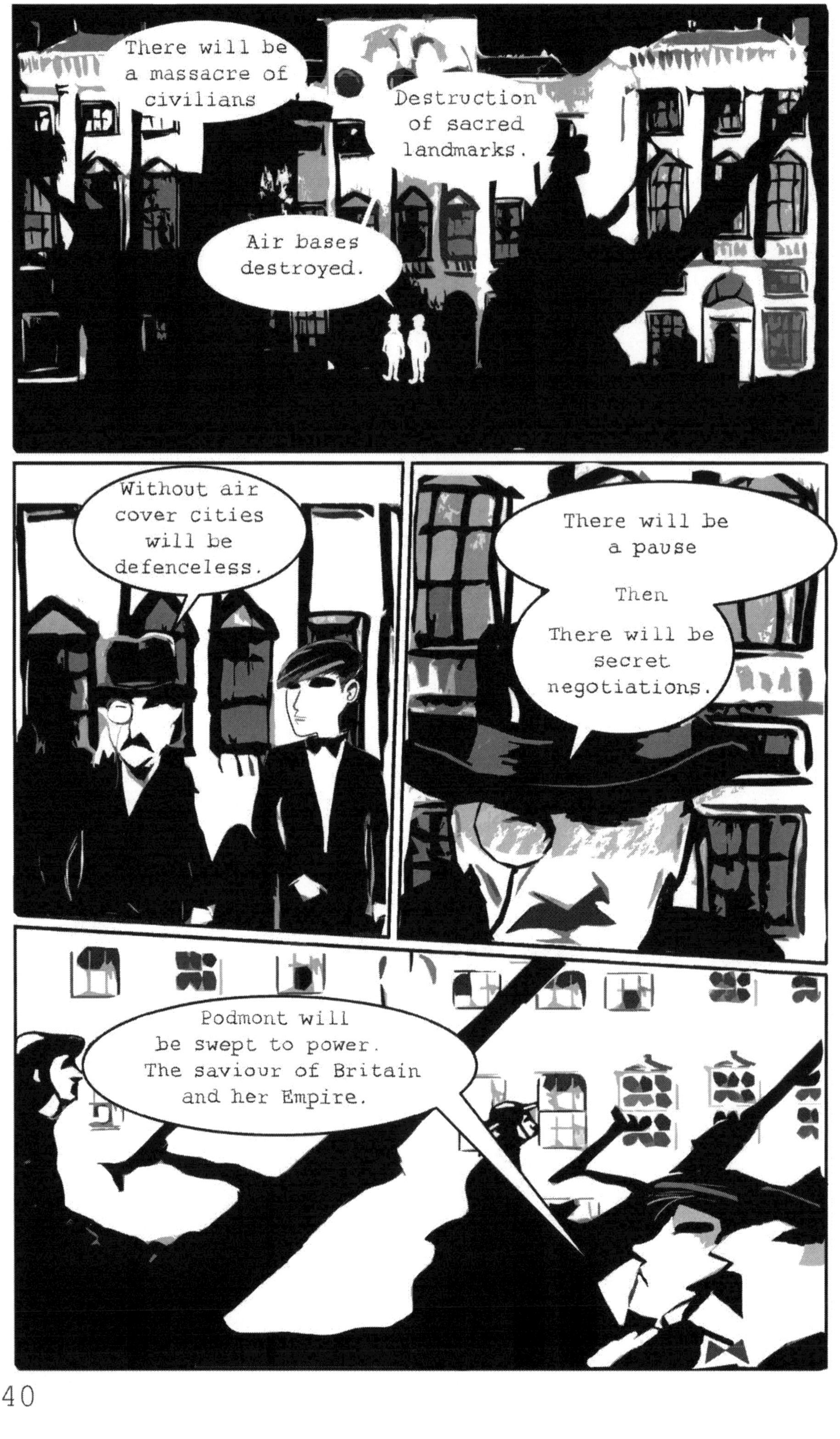

There will be a massacre of civilians

Destruction of sacred landmarks.

Air bases destroyed.

Without air cover cities will be defenceless.

There will be a pause

Then

There will be secret negotiations.

Congratulations.
It seems to me that your planning has been faultless.
All you need do is wait a few days...
...and everything will just fall into your hands.
Alas, there is still some tweaking to be done.
The things that make him popular with our foreign, erm, allies can still make him suspect here.
Our public love him as a world champion driver and constructor of a world beating car.
We now need to emphasise him as an English gentleman. A symbol of all the best qualities of the nation and its empire.
A representative of all that is great in our pure Anglo-Saxon culture.
I, of course, have a plan that requires your expertise.

Of course one must not forget the cultural contribution he has made to the nation. His patronage of all the arts has been considerable.
He's certainly hounded out all those avant garde leftists.

His taste is conservative
Classical not "modern"
Shares public preference for the conventional.

I fail to see how I can be of any use to you.

That's easy
You are going to propose marriage to Stella Podmont.

One minor flaw
She doesn't like me

What on earth has that got to do with anything? She's rich and we're powerful End of story!
Father admit it, she hates me!

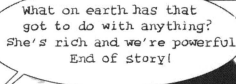

She may be the richest heiress in England.

PODMONT STATION, KENT, 30 MINUTES FROM WATERLOO.

The engagement will be announced with maximum fanfare.
Aren't there certain formalities to be observed?
We will pay full respect to the solemnity of the moment.

What if the fair maid refuses her ardent suitor?
That is not an option.

Father, Couldn't you, at least, have given me some notice?
Son, this is the age of the Blitzkrieg.
We must move with the times.

Mighty King Arthur! Your Saintly knights await to do your bidding.

Hail! Unworthy Subjects!
Descend O mighty one! Favour us with thine presence!

The air is full of expensive perfume.
Dear Lord, do you know who gave me this cigar?

You're not trying to make me jealous? Hasn't he resigned yet?

I see you've brought the handsome prince.
I do hope the Princess is better disposed to an Abbey wedding?
The nation needs a show of pagentry...
To tell who's in charge.
It's like a marriage between ourselves Podmont!

No pretence. I'll do what I can to help father.
I trained as an actress and for me this is just another temporary role.
Not going too well, Stevens?
Leonard's a duffer at girls.
Smouldering stare
?
baleful glare
In the circumstances that may be a very good thing.
She can act the adoring wife, he can look dashing.
We'll leave you two young things together whilst we two old fogies gossip about boring issues.
My horse needs a canter.
The ministerial boxes require my attention.
Lady Stella will do her duty. But no more.

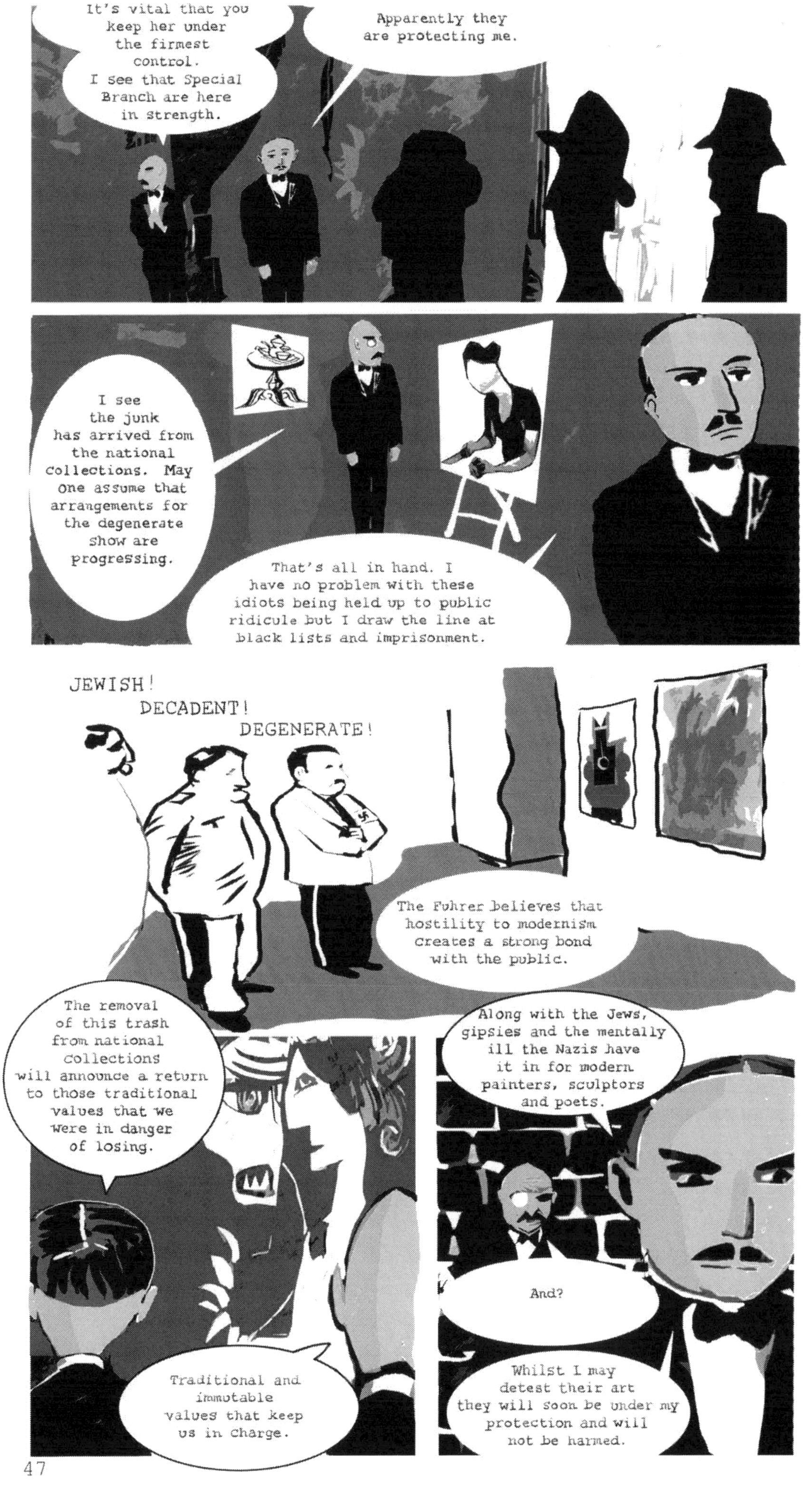

JEWISH!
DECADENT!
DEGENERATE!

The Fuhrer believes that hostility to modernism creates a strong bond with the public.

The removal of this trash from national collections will announce a return to those traditional values that we were in danger of losing.

Traditional and immutable values that keep us in charge.

Along with the Jews, gipsies and the mentally ill the Nazis have it in for modern painters, sculptors and poets.

And?

Whilst I may detest their art they will soon be under my protection and will not be harmed.

Library's bugged but your study is safe.

You need a bloody lift old boy!
puff
puff

Might rather spoil the medieval ambiance.
Bugger the ambiance! Sometimes I wish you were a modernist.

Here is the actual reason for my popularity. The sporting champion. The Podmont myth.
A hero today is forgotten tomorrow Act quickly or the magic will be gone.

No one comes in here. Not even Stella.
Look through the private pictures I've sorted for your people.

Just assume that you are always spied upon.
In the wrong hands these images could ruin us.

Surely race victories can do me nothing but good.
It's the company you keep.

Hob nobbing with Hitler on the eve of invasion isn't a good look.
But once he's received in Whitehall as our ally against the Russian menace they'll be most welcome.

I believe that image may haunt me forever.

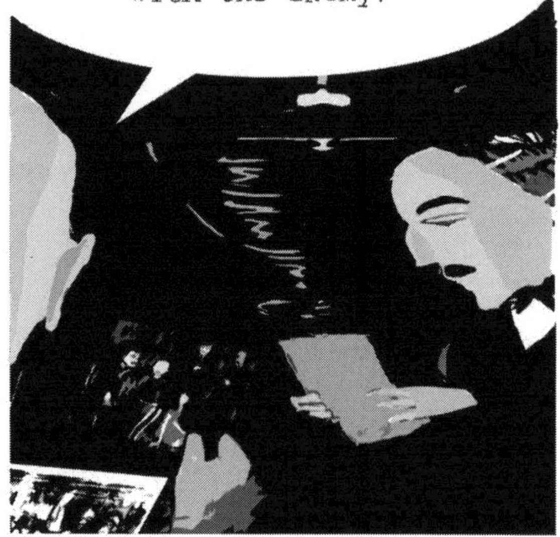
Podmont, there's another one here of you posing with the enemy.

Taken here. In your very own home.

Everyone knows the role the Severinis play in the race team.
The car is their creation.

My sources inform me that the family are still here and enjoy your full protection.
By harbouring enemy aliens you are committing a serious criminal offence.

Commanding view you have from up here Podmont old boy.
You can see right into the walled garden.
Come away Stevens.

Right on cue enters wop junior.
I can sense an assignation.
He has a name. Vincenzo.

Come away Stevens. Leave him in peace.

Hang on! This is getting lively. He's being joined by a young lady.
Stevens, we're in the midst of a national crisis!

Damned pretty filly she is too!
Hold on! Isn't that the delectable Stella?

GOOD GOD!
And she's smiling at the young rogue!
Man, do you realise that your engaged daughter is smiling at an enemy alien.

Just what is going on here Podmont?

SHIT!

Don't tell me you didn't know about this!

Podmont, this place is swarming with professional spies all reporting to MI5
Christ almighty! This is catastrophic!
Podmont! Sit down and listen. For once in your life you are going to hear some mature words.

First of all let us remind ourselves of the facts.
Italy cunningly waited until the fall of France before entering the war on the winning side
Collar all Italian residents!
Then Winston, characteristically, took swift revenge.
fish and chips
fish and chips
Then, of course, the mob turned on the defenceless.
MANY HAVE BEEN SHIPPED ABROAD
And now, your lordship, it is time to act.

God's teeth! They're still at it.

You know this could be curtains for our whole operation unless you pull your finger out.

The Severinis are here under my protection. I have a moral responsibility for them. I refuse to hand them back and forth like cattle.

Listen to me you pampered aristocrat!

From here you will leave major decisions to me. The Severinis go tonight!

I love these people!
This is where you stop being a dilletante and act like a responsible leader

You will order this family's immediate arrest and deportation.

Podmont here. I require you to remove two male enemy aliens squatting in my estate lodge.

Apparently his lordship has requested that we be discrete.

Discrete
but
firm.

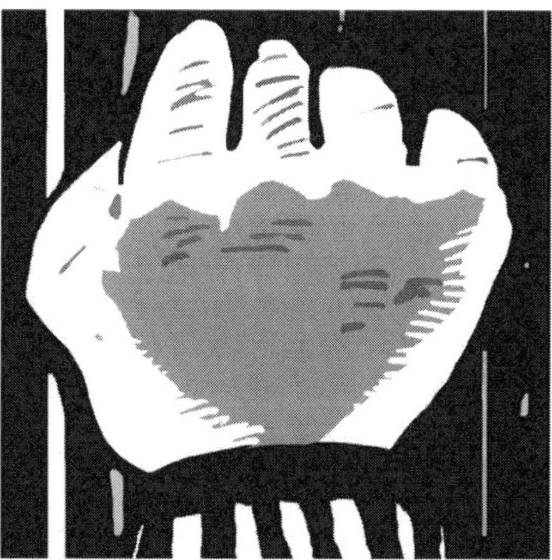

RATATAT
ATATAT
AT

Is Lord Podmont aware of this?

Who do you think tipped us off Luigi?

The Arandora Star
Birkenhead on Merseyside.
June 30th 1940

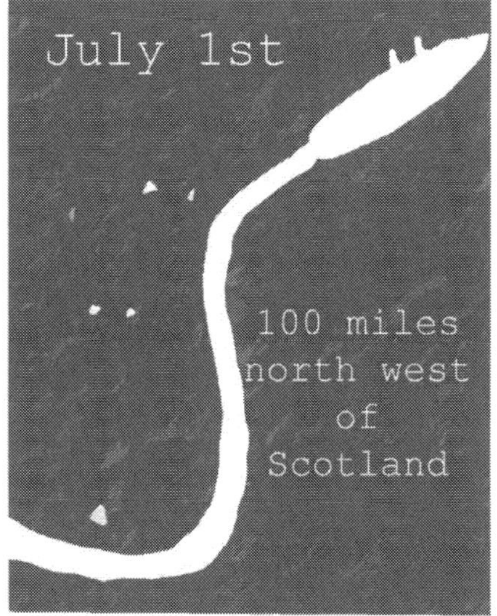
July 1st
100 miles north west of Scotland

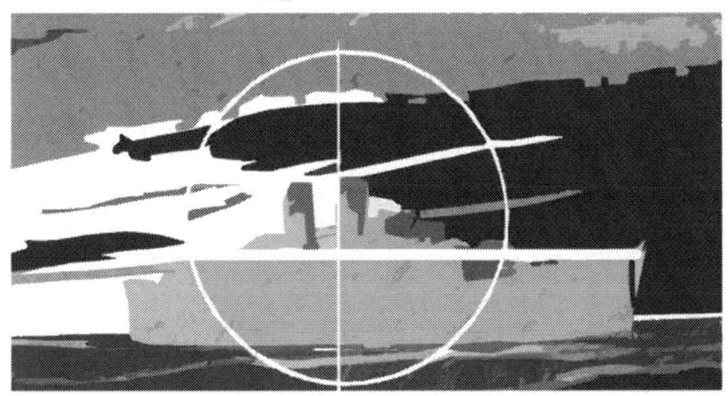

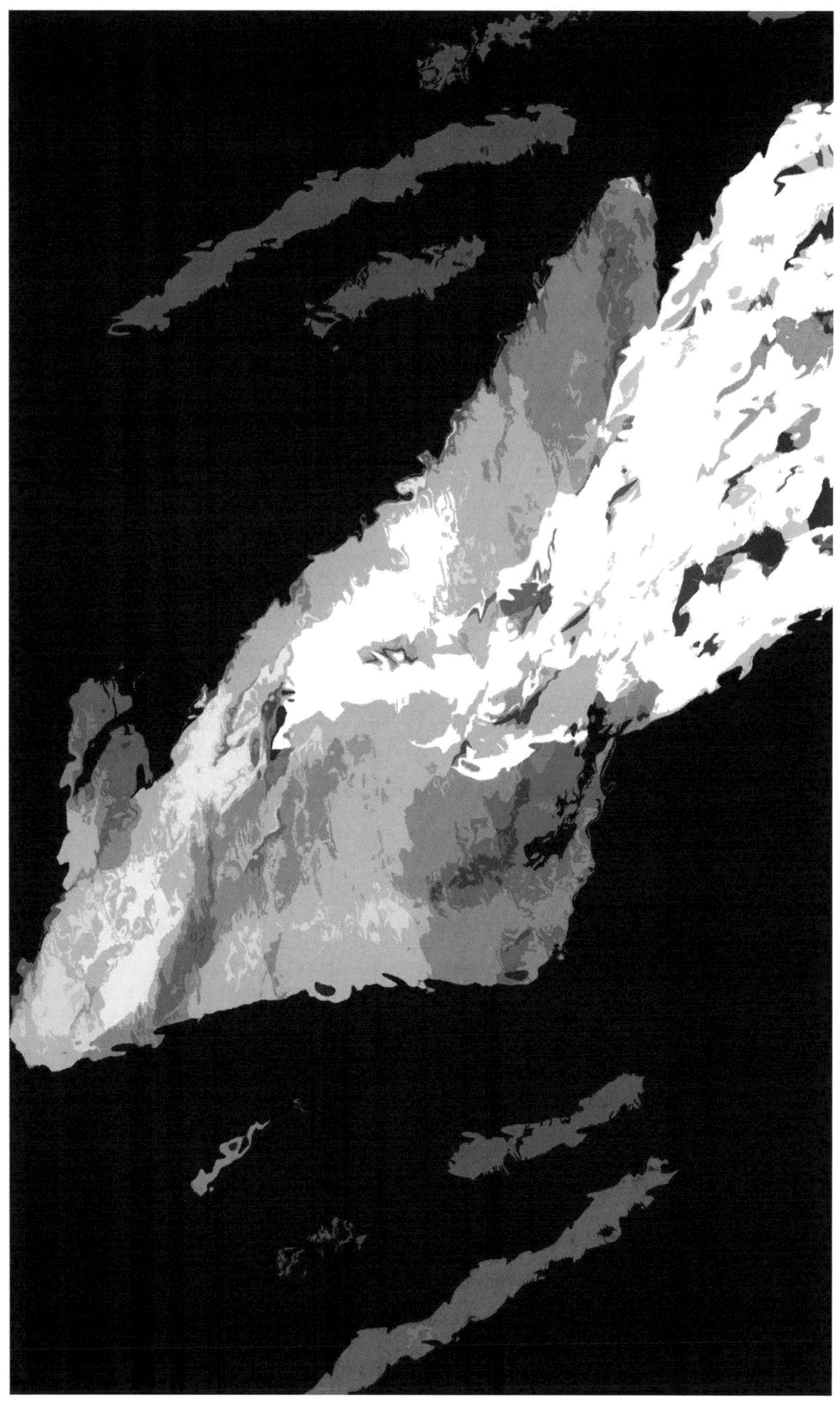

KABOOM

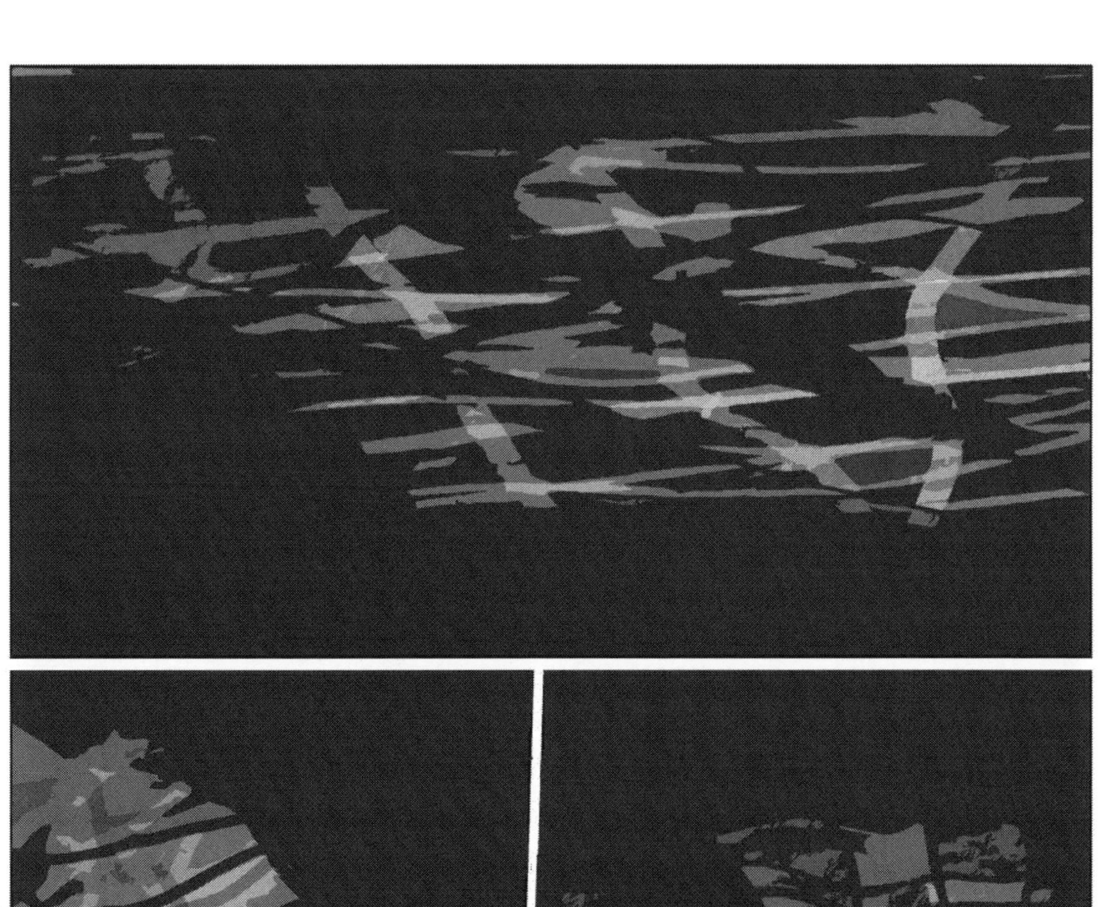

I have news.

Vincenzo has been picked up. There is no hope for Antonio.

How long before Vincenzo is returned to us? He will be tired and unwell.

All survivors are to be reassigned to other ships. Winston wants rid of them.

I will speak to father. He must do something.

Today I no longer have the power. Stella, my dear, these are fast moving times. Before you rush to judgment listen to my story.

Only yesterday Sir John was haranguing Winston again. Making demands that would ease our way into power. Winston, at last, seemed to realise that his support in the party was melting away and events had moved beyond his control..... when

Important message from admiralty sir!
news came that a Royal Naval force was sitting along side the French fleet just off the coast of Africa awaiting instructions.
Following the French capitulation there was a real fear that the French fleet would be tamely passed to the axis powers and its guns turned on our ships in the Mediterranean.
An immediate decision was required.

I insist you do nothing rash. Tomorrow the government will be changed utterly.
Britain will fight until the end.

FIRE!!!

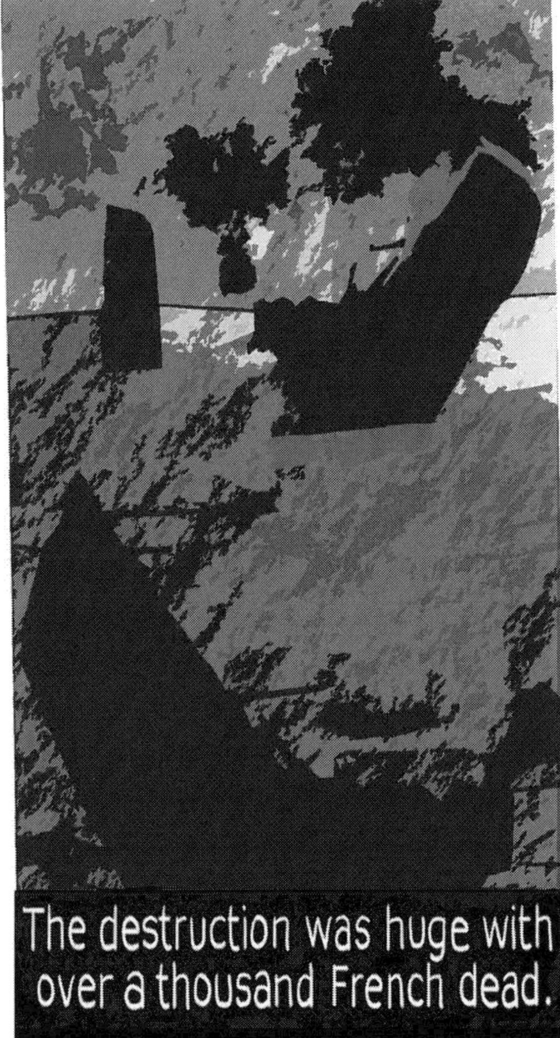
The destruction was huge with over a thousand French dead.

At a stroke Winston has banished all doubt and doubters Britain's people and parliament have fallen in behind him united in the crazy belief that they can win. It's magnificent but stark mad.

So from the brink
of absolute power
I am but a prisoner
in my own home.

From here on
things are done
my way.

All contacts with
Germany and
Italy have been
declared
acts of treason.

Many of our
supporters have
been arrested.

Party members have
universally swung
behind him.

Winston's is the only
show in town.

So you see, my dear child, there is absolutely nothing I can do to save anyone.
England will indeed go down fighting.
And what about the great Sir John?

Whilst I have been dropped Stevens' powers of enforcement are still much in demand.

So just when it was most needed and could do the most good

all the power has gone out of this great house.

Stella has no peace.
Not even in dreams.

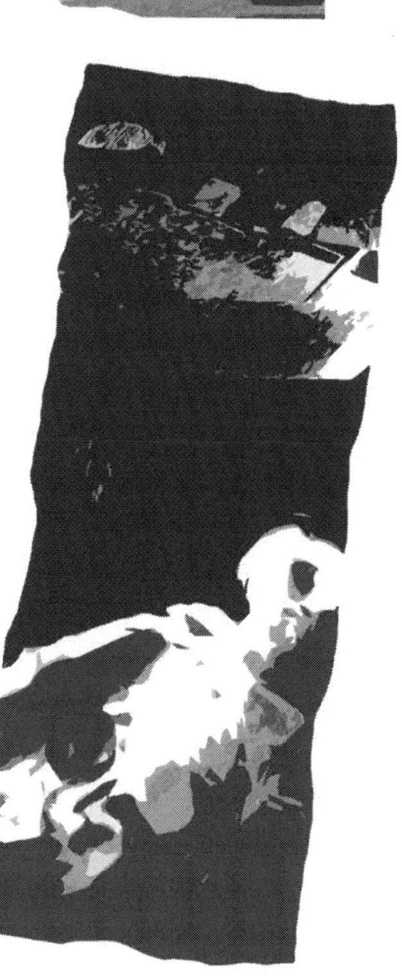

Stella awakens to a pale, cold dawn and feels utterly alone.

Kindly inform the minister that Lady Podmont urgently needs to discuss an issue of great importance.

Young lady, Sir John is concerned with the gravest emergency this country has faced and will speak to nobody at present.

O dear! That is rather regrettable as it means I must take my story to the police and to a few of daddy's editor friends....
No, I don't mind holding on for a few moments.

Sir John, we must do all we can to aid Vincenzo Severini.

I am doing all I can to limit the damage that young man has done to your family's reputation. You and your father have been severely compromised.

You must let an older and wiser head than your own deal with these issues You must have things to occupy your mind. Ponies to exercise, shopping to do.

I am prepared to do or say whatever is necessary to save Vincenzo. We have already murdered his father and tortured his family This must stop.

I would caution you against making threats. State precisely what you want and be realistic. There's a bloody war on.

I want a destination, date and tickets. I want assurances about Vincenzo's treatment and safety.

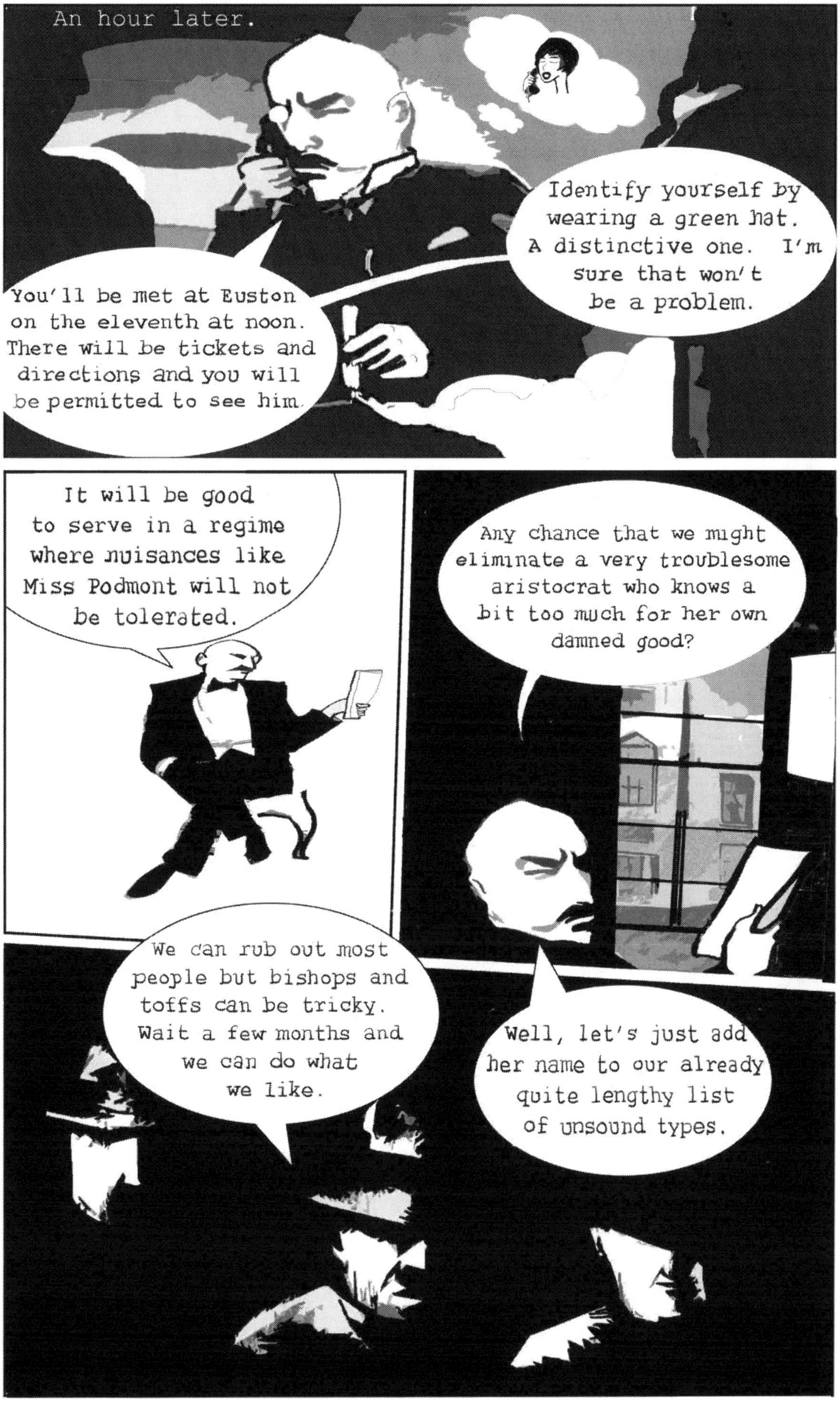

It will be good to serve in a regime where nuisances like Miss Podmont will not be tolerated.

Any chance that we might eliminate a very troublesome aristocrat who knows a bit too much for her own damned good?

We can rub out most people but bishops and toffs can be tricky. Wait a few months and we can do what we like.

Well, let's just add her name to our already quite lengthy list of unsound types.

..they're items of documentation that will keep you safe from Stevens' machinations.

Identity cards! According to these I'm a government agent!

In the event of an invasion Winston expects us all to go underground and lead the resistance. Even me.
Sometimes I think he's looking forward to it.

Stella, I'm just so sorry for all that's happened. Can I ever be forgiven?
Just a pity that you didn't stand up to Sir John earlier. It is him I can't forgive.
How can he sleep knowing he turned two innocent men in? Sending one of them to his death

I think that man will cast a shadow over my life for ever.

And nothing in your past has prepared you for the danger I've now placed you in.

One unintended consequence of Winston's attempt to humiliate me
is that I have been directed to finance a small resistance group on the north west coast.
My subordinates have reliably informed me that Vincenzo will depart on a ship called the Dunera and you will be met by one of our female agents who will provide access to the dock side.

You will still need Stevens for transport and documents giving you access to Vincenzo but that is all.

Don't liase with Stevens' agents beyond London. You will be met by my agent on route to the port.
But trust no one. You will always be in extreme peril.

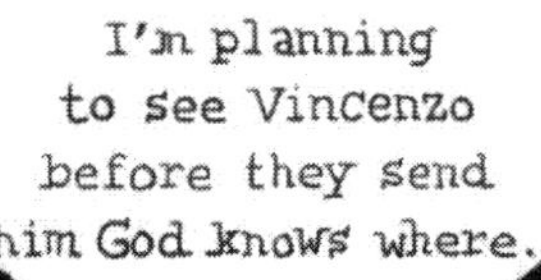
I'm planning
to see Vincenzo
before they send
him God knows where.

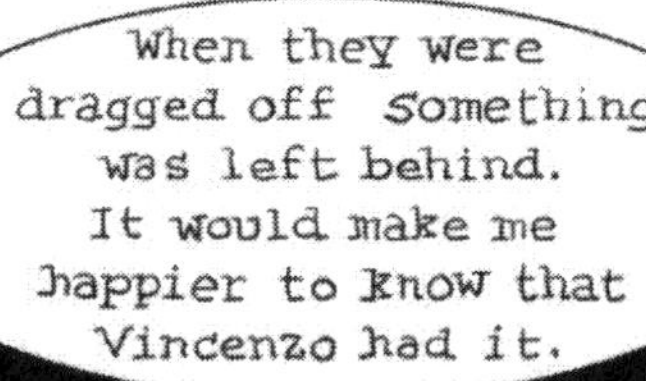
When they were
dragged off something
was left behind.
It would make me
happier to know that
Vincenzo had it.

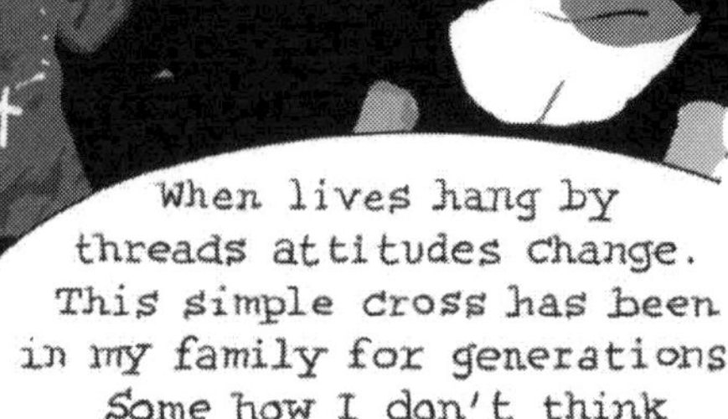

A crucifix?
I didn't know you
were a religious family.

When lives hang by
threads attitudes change.
This simple cross has been
in my family for generations.
Some how I don't think
it will end up on the
ocean's floor.

There are stories
attached to it. It
first came to us
long ago in the rugged
mountains that lie
between Rome and Napoli

The story goes...
In the town
below a convent
lived a girl
of flawless beauty.

She was much loved
by all who knew her.
Her mother protected
her from the evil eye
in the old way.

Always she
was pursued by the
town's eligible
young men. All
enchanted by her
many gifts

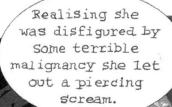

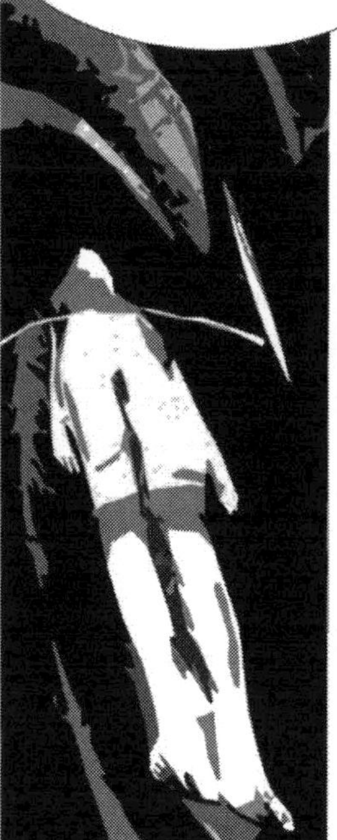
Until one night
she was awoken
from deep sleep
by a searing pain.

Her flesh, usually
as smooth as silk
was roughened by
blisters and warts.

Realising she
was disfigured by
some terrible
malignancy she let
out a piercing
scream.

She attempted to carry on as before. But everywhere she went...

It was a time of plague when whole communities could be wiped off the earth's face.

Fear of contagion grew and she was taken into the seclusion of the convent above.

It was believed that death would soon claim her.

All that was left was prayer for salvation.

She remembered loved ones and waited.

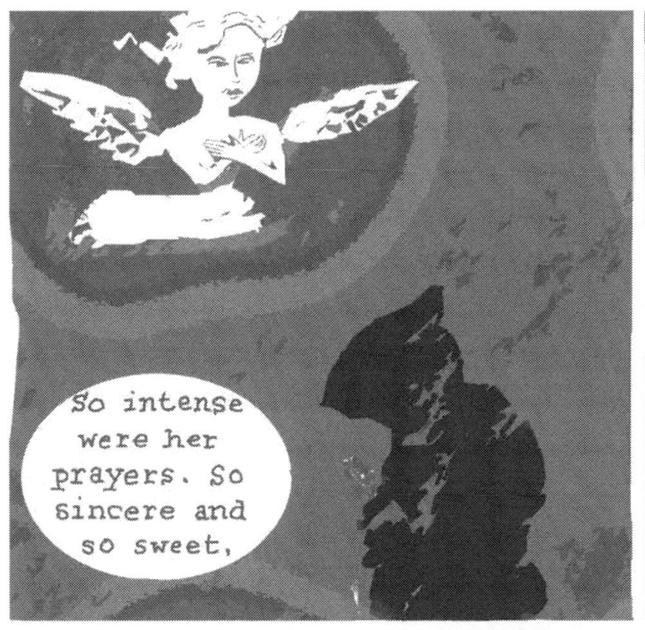
So intense were her prayers. So sincere and so sweet,

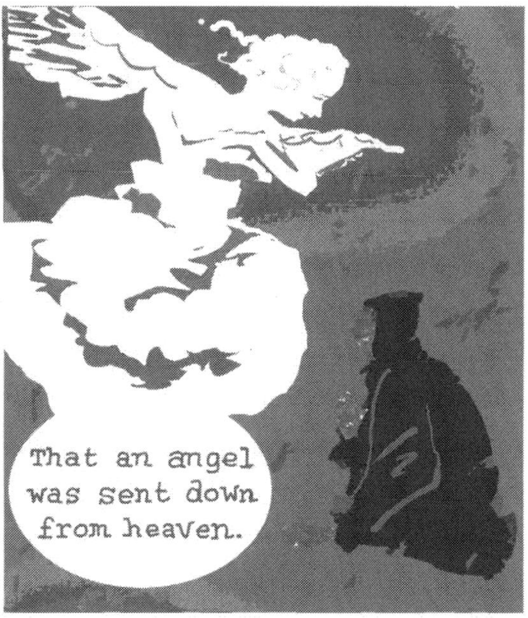
That an angel was sent down from heaven.

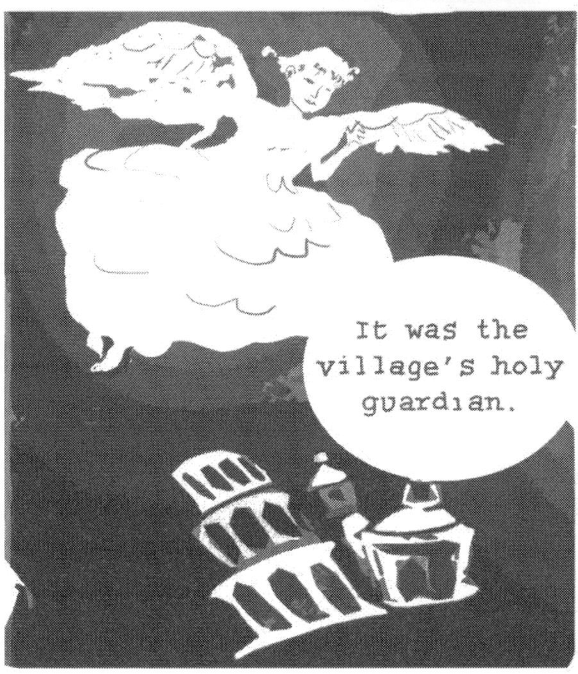
It was the village's holy guardian.

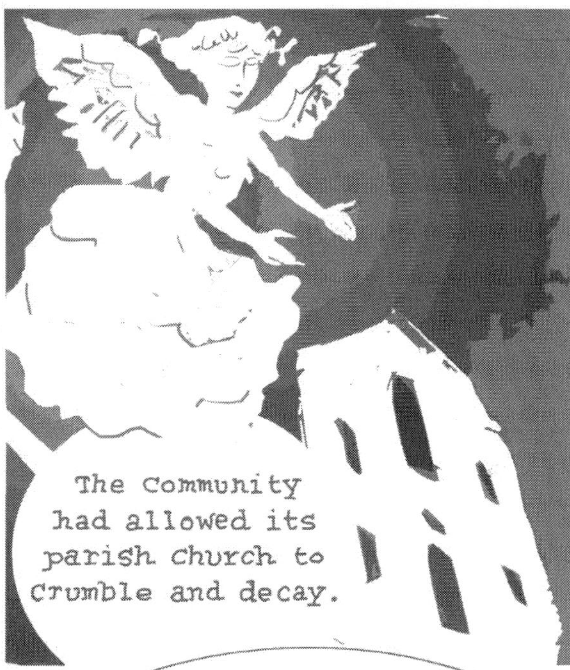
The Community had allowed its parish Church to Crumble and decay.

The angel had a plan for its restoration. A miracle was to be announced.
To the jaded villagers announcements of miracles meant demands for funds but news of sudden loss and restoration of physical beauty could not be ignored.

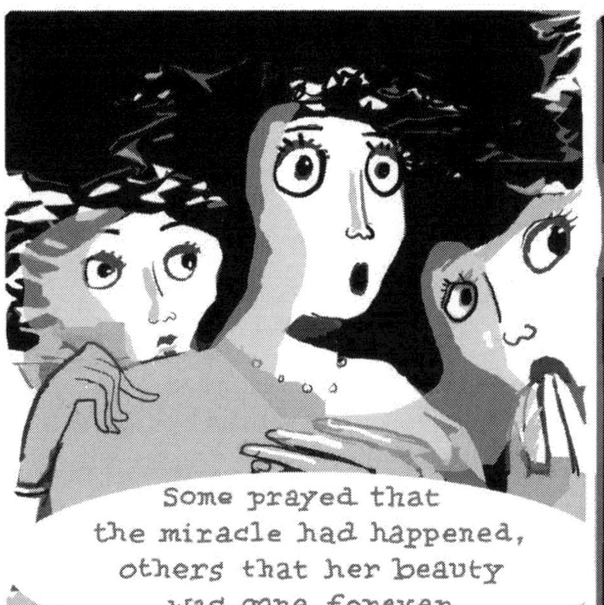
Some prayed that
the miracle had happened,
others that her beauty
was gone forever.

The girl threw
back her cloak
and revealed her
unblemished
face.
Imagine the
gasps and the
sense of awe...

..at powers that could rob and
restore a woman's treasured gifts
in such a random and ruthless way.
Never had a restoration
project been started
with such enthusiasm
and done in record time.

For her faith
and courage a
gift was made.
The cross worn
by the order's
founding saint.
And the
promise of
protection in
time of peril.

Only for it to tumble unnoticed on the floor...
...at just the moment when its power was most needed.
Perhaps you can understand why I might be so concerned that Vincenzo would wear it when he sets out on so dangerous a journey.

You must
wear it!

I'm honoured.

Like the
hat?
***

eloquent!

Like my
hat?
Most
practical
my lady.

Euston noon 11th July

Here are tickets
and map. He's on
The Dunera. She
sails tomorrow.

Release papers for
Vincenzo Severini?
Where are they?

Has no one told you
that we're at war
with bloody Italy.

Spoilt bitch!

Don't tell me darlin, your hubby's an admiral ain't he?
Of course. He's on The Dunera.
Blimey! Don't expect him home before Christmas.

Taxi for the dock side my good man.
There'll be no taxis tonight luv.

But if you wait a while I'll walk you over there myself. There's a short cut through the wood.
Thanks for the kind offer. But if you could just give me directions I'll be on my way.

sSSSSSSSSSSSSSS
ssssssssSSSSSSSS
SSSSSSSSSSSSSSSSSSSSssssssssssssssssssssss

russle

shriek

crackle!

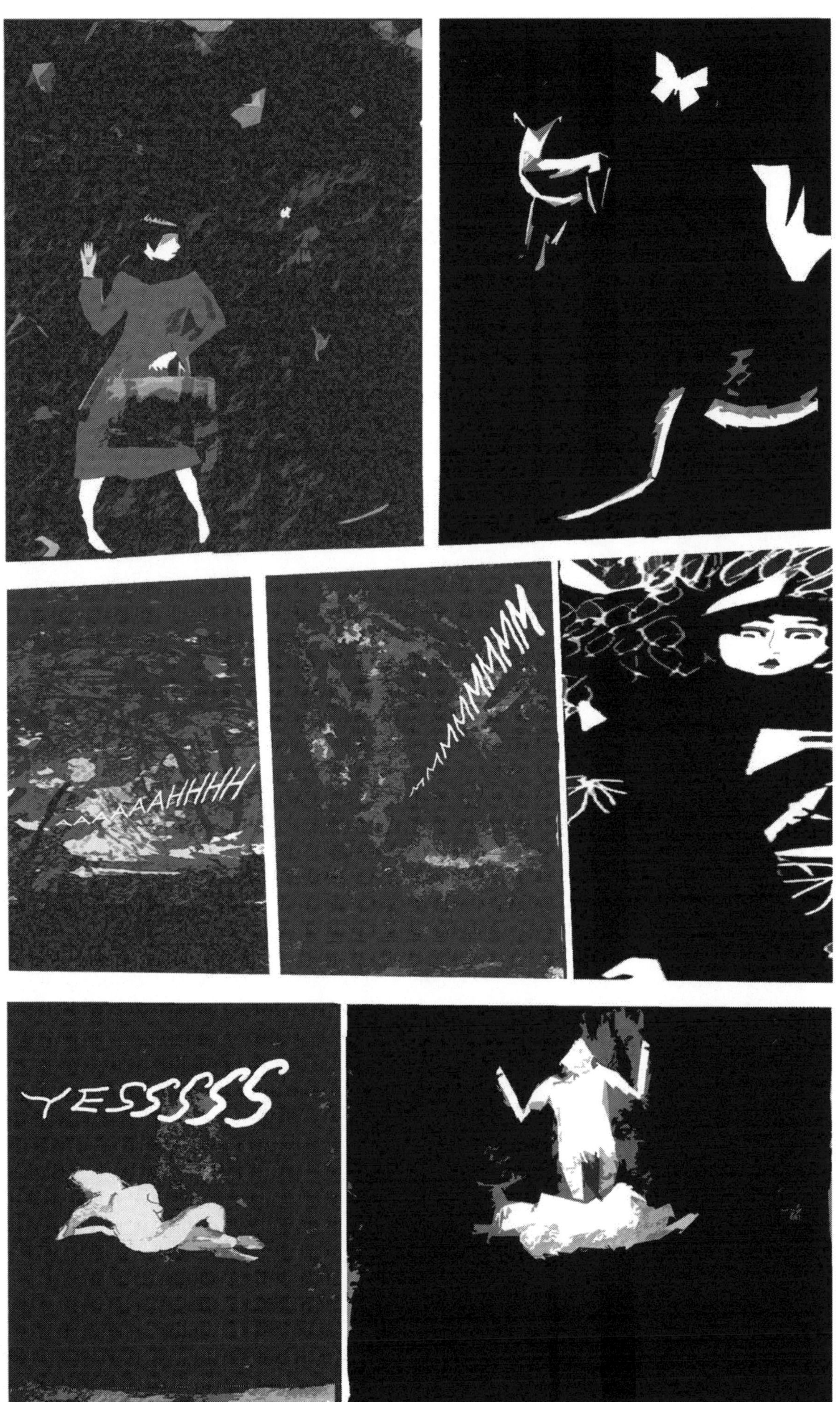
AAAAAAAHHHHH
MMMMMMMMMMMM
YESSSSSS

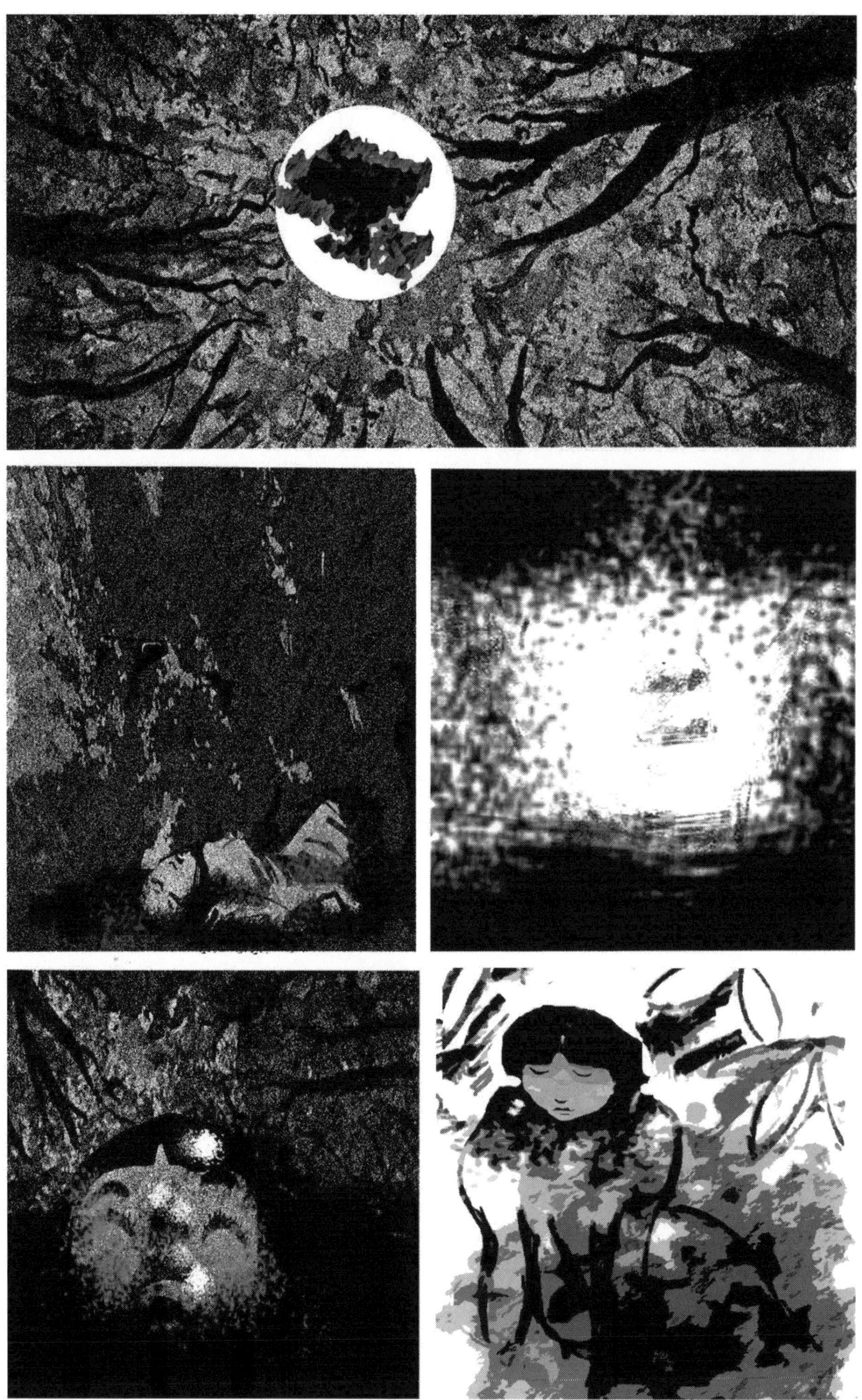

MY GOD!

I give up.
Whoever you are,
you can do your worst

If you don't mind me saying so darling your boobs are a bit on the small side.

Might I ask what you're doing out here in the middle of nowhere dressed in very little apart from stolen underwear?
Once the Nasties arrive we'll all have to get used to life in the wild.

I'm afraid I'm just a lost girl. I'm not used to wild places in the middle of the night. I would appreciate it if you would guide me to the port. I have an appointment to keep.

How do I look?
You must teach me how to do your injured child act.

Lovely bits of satin dear. You've got the most fantastic taste for a lost girl. I've been through your papers. Most impressive they are too. Lady Podmont.

I am currently a government agent on work of national importance.
You're welcome to all of my stuff. I hope you enjoy it.

A girl needs something soft next to her skin.
Winston needs tarts as well as toffs. He wants to infiltrate the enemy at all levels.
You can keep everything. It's all of no importance. All I require are my papers and ....
....my cross.
That cross is most special. Give it back and I can complete my mission.
Without the cross I cannot continue.

How do I know these papers aren't cunning forgeries? You don't look tough enough to be a resistance fighter.

You'll see how tough I am if you don't support me in gaining the release of the undercover agent on The Dunera.

Why should some wop geezer act for England when his lot are on the point of winning the bloody war?

At this stage of the proceedings I don't care what you believe. Just give me the cross.

Whoever you are
think of the cross
as the toll
you must pay
to cross my land

I am one of
nature's aristocrats
The forest's
queen. Do what I
command...
or else!

I am queen of the fairies.
Daughter of the Frog Prince.
You will obey me!

Your word is my
command
your majesty.

I see this cross
is a thing of the
highest value.
A magic love token.

But my father is a
wealthy man.
You will be handsomely
rewarded for its
surrender.

I'm a spoilt little rich girl who had the benefits of the very best education that money could buy.

Once upon a time in a land far, far away.

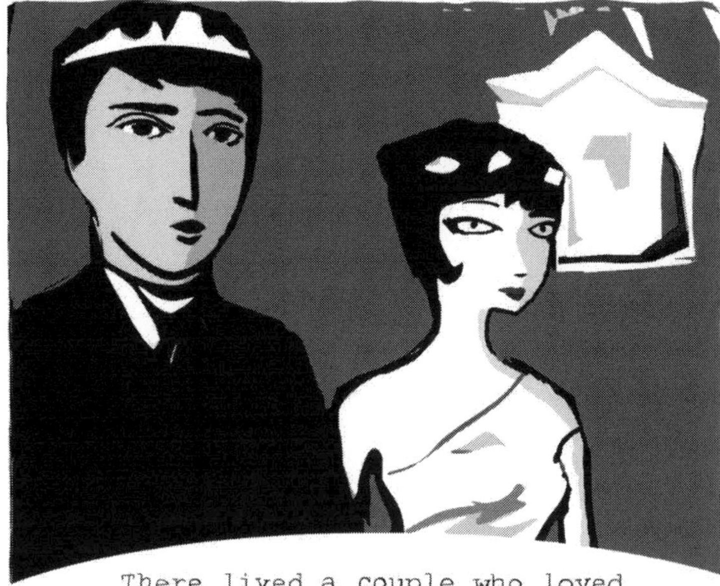
There lived a couple who loved each other very much. She was called Alcyon he was called Ceyx.

Just how much did your classical education cost? Let's have more detail please.
There's no need to tell me he's handsome and she's beautiful.

Who's telling this story anyway?
They were quite attractive as it happens!

Why not just say they were beautiful then?

Such was their love
for each other...

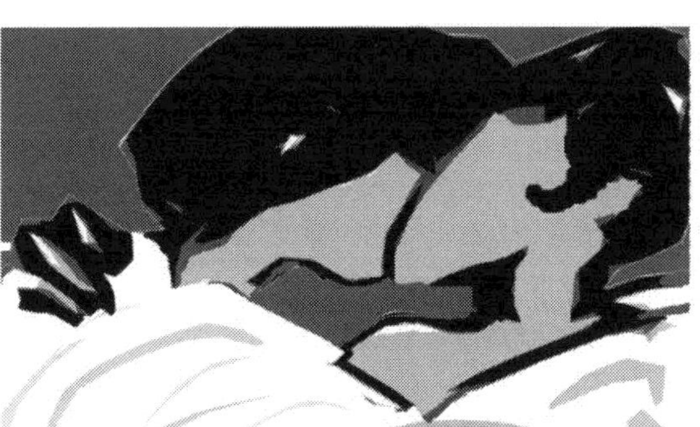
They so longed to be
in the arms of the other.

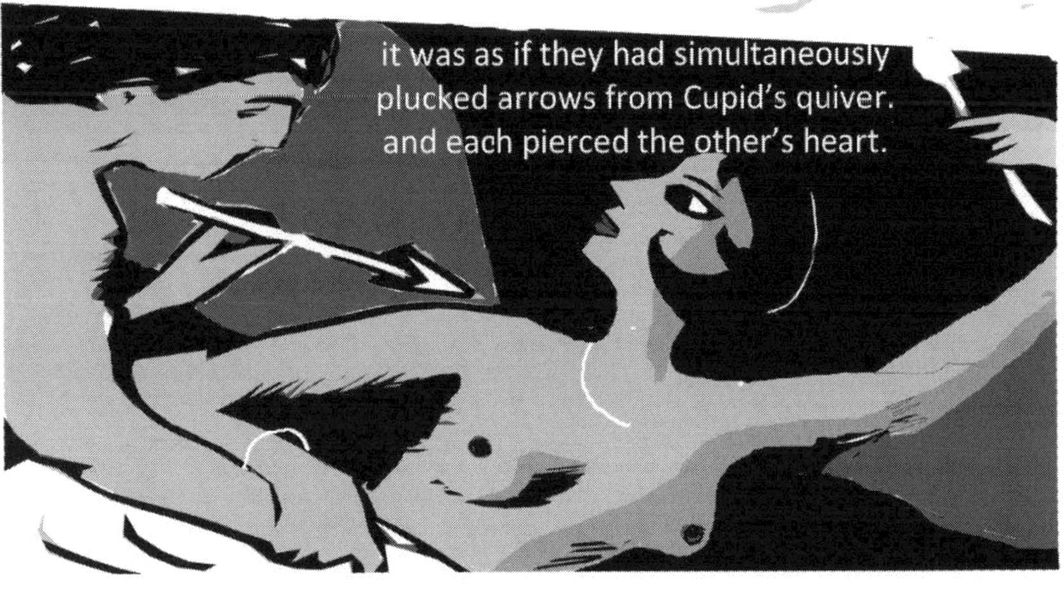
it was as if they had simultaneously
plucked arrows from Cupid's quiver.
and each pierced the other's heart.

To their adoring subjects they were like giants, even gods.
But with great power came great responsibility.

Royal duty dictated that Prince Ceyx should undertake a dangerous journey.
I must sail to the oracle at Delphi.
I shall share the danger.
Remain here and I promise to return in one month.
Why have I such a bad feeling about this trip?

For many years they had never been apart. But the call of duty could not be ignored.

How little things have changed!

The Prince has seen his people struck by hunger and disease. He must consult the oracle and make sacrifice to the Gods.
As the time for departure approached Alcyon felt increasing dread.

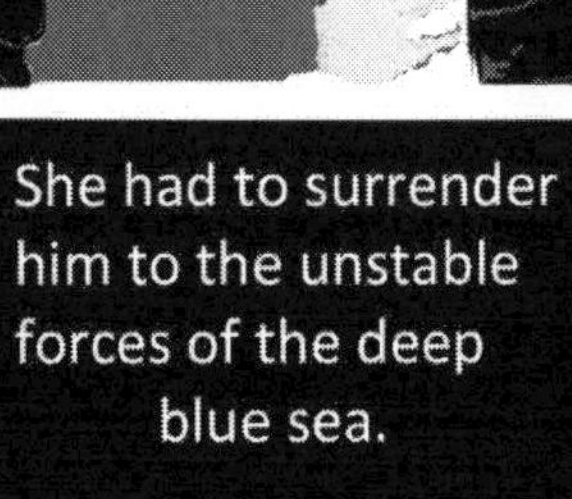
She had to surrender him to the unstable forces of the deep blue sea.

Whilst she might still be seen from the departing boat she hid her tears.

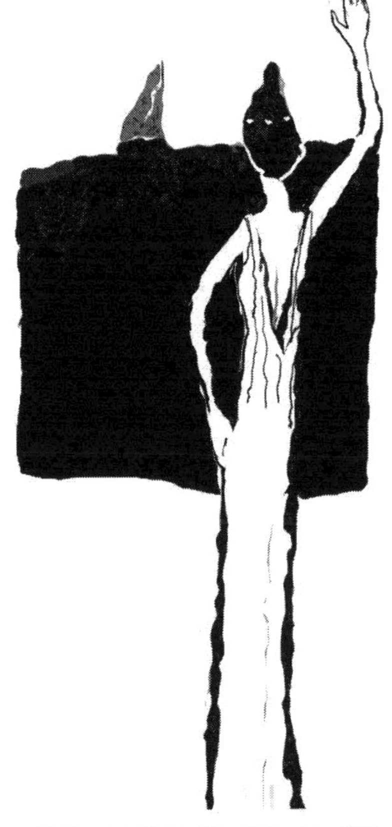
By the moment of the the ship's disapperance over the earth's rim she was already praying.

At first the boat makes good speed powered by a steady wind. But how soon that breeze became a storm and the storm a gale until it became a.....

HURRICANE

How thrilling! What about the sailors?

They tried all they knew to save their ship. Were finally forced to admit defeat,

They thought of home.
They prayed then....

They went down to their doom.

To lie forever with their stricken ship on the ocean's rocky floor.

I'm not sure I like this story!
What happens next?

What about her beloved "Princey"?

As Alcyon had feared. The ocean claimed her lover's life. Now as she waited for his return he was already beyond any need of protection.

His final thoughts were all with Alcyon. He only hoped that by some miracle his body might be transported home so that he might share his tomb with his beloved when her time to join him finally came.

It was as if he called to Alcyon in her dreams. Even though she sensed the tragedy had already happened she still clung to the fragile shreds of hope.

In the days that followed Alcyon experienced many visions. She had difficulty distinguishing between wakefulness and sleep. One night she trapped a raven believing it to be a messenger from the gods. Then moved by its piteous croaks of despair she gave it its freedom.

So strong was her
lover's presence that
she sensed it
everywhere.

The palace seemed
haunted by some
restless spirit.

Outside every
door and window.
It was as if
he were waiting
to be invited
in by someone
who spoke the
dialect of the dead.

Alcyon had
become a
form of spectre
haunting her
own home.
Starved of sleep,
food and
above all of
love.

In her heart she
knew the truth.
But she was still
tortured by a
lingering hope.

She prayed that her
faith in a
compassionate universe
might not fade away.

The gods were shamed
by the hopelessness of her
prayers and decided to send
a messenger to confirm the truth.

In the depths of the darkest night Alcyon awakes with a start, suddenly aware of a dark and menacing presence in her chamber.

How horrible! This is too scary!

I'll never sleep in the dark again. Not alone anyway!

The God of Sleep has sent his son, Morpheus the Shapeshifter, in the form of the living prince. Whilst his voice is kindly he presents the facts of the prince's death. Alcyon ,at last, accepts the truth but begs to be allowed to join her husband in death.

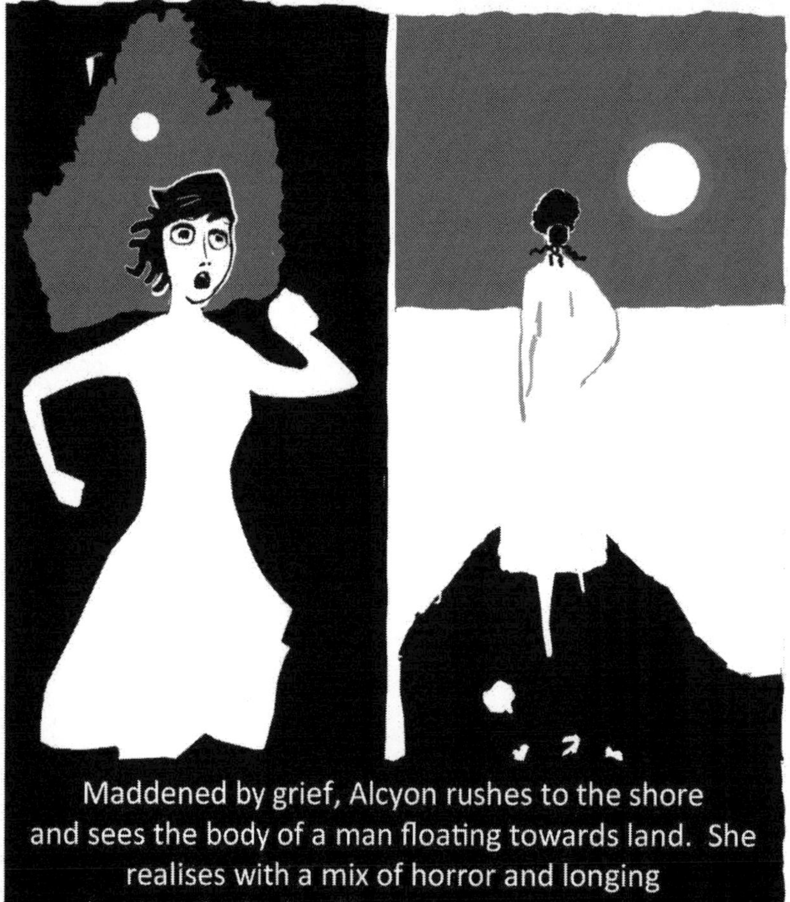

Maddened by grief, Alcyon rushes to the shore and sees the body of a man floating towards land. She realises with a mix of horror and longing that it is the body of her Prince returning home.

But darling you're crying. This story means that much to you?

It means the world to me. Give me the cross and I'll stop.

Don't you dare! Just get on with it. What happens next?

She approaches the cliff edge.

She contemplates the drop.
She dives

But just before impact and certain death she soars above the waves.

Seeing her distress the Gods show pity. As she approaches him her lover stirs.

As two seabirds the lovers are reunited and soar high above the stormy seas. Only becalmed once each year at the intervention of Poseidon.

And so in that form the lovers could live on and again enjoy the great passion they had shared before.
The end.

I wasn't expecting such a sad story.

I do find the story strangely comforting.

Lovely darling, though I think I'd prefer it without feathers.

To have love and happiness snatched away is so cruel.

Here's your cross. Dry those eyes and let's go find that prince.
Even if he's just one of those sad Italian boys.

The tide is high Sky's clear and the ship won't wait long.
I'm a bloomin' romantic!

Follow me!

Ten minutes later.
What is that infernal noise?
You'll soon see.
Just poke that aristocratic head through the gap in the hedge.
Good Gracious! What a drop!

I know it looks steep, but if you shut up and follow my lead....
But I've no head for heights.
There must be a safer route. A path, stairs or a road....... you'd need a parachute or wings.
Think of romance. Think of Alcyon.
There's no time for safety. The tide is in and the ship is setting sail.
This is not a story it's really real.
Watch me as I spin three times and listen for the magic word.
GERONIMO

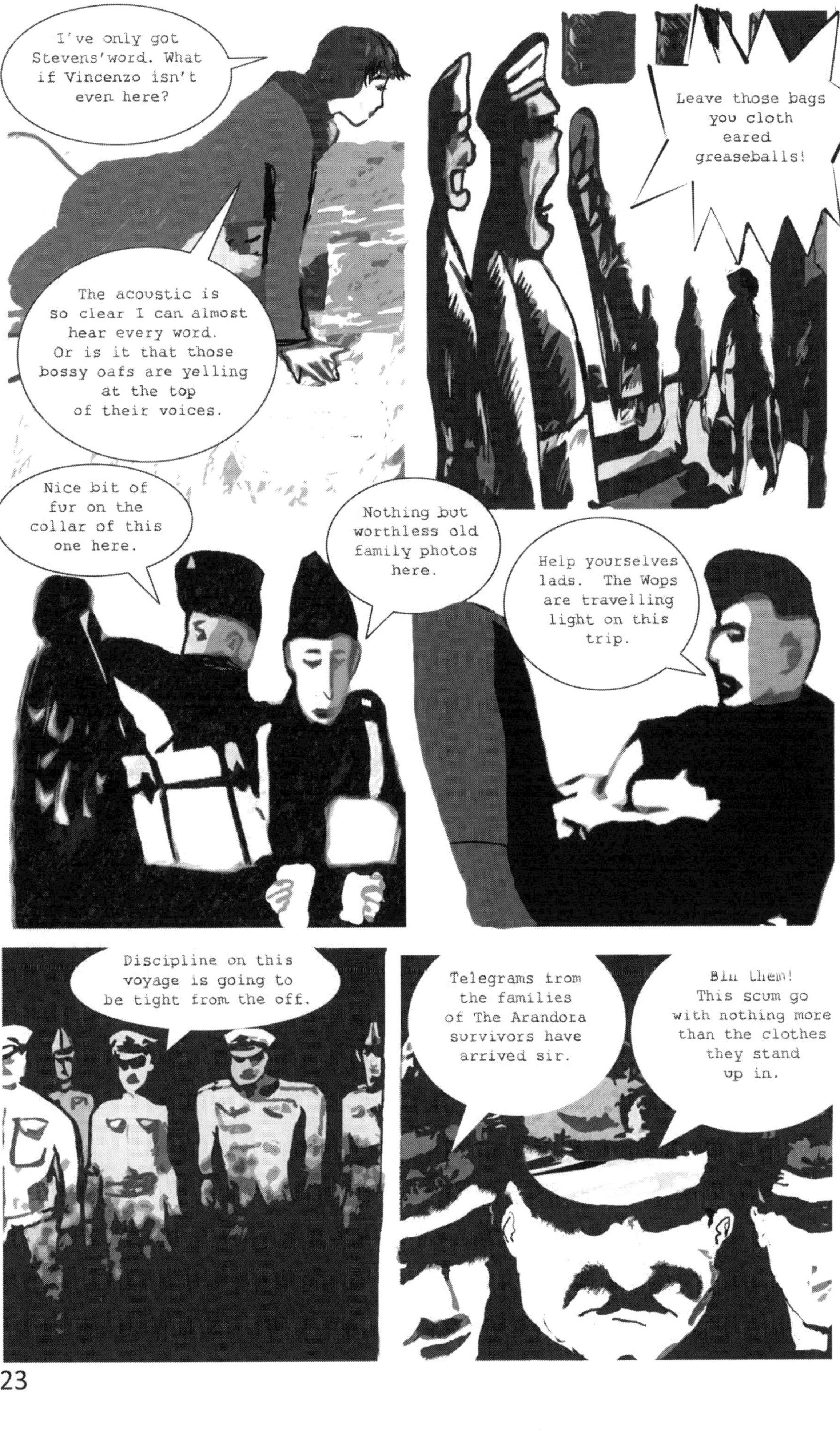

I've only got Stevens'word. What if Vincenzo isn't even here?

Leave those bags you cloth eared greaseballs!

The acoustic is so clear I can almost hear every word. Or is it that those bossy oafs are yelling at the top of their voices.

Nice bit of fur on the collar of this one here.

Nothing but worthless old family photos here.

Help yourselves lads. The Wops are travelling light on this trip.

I cannot believe what I'm seeing down there.

They can't be treating prisoners that way! Good God! We're English.

Move your arse Princess! There's no time to spare.
These boys are willing to turn a blind eye.
But it's such a drop!
Remember your promise! Remember the cross!
If I could only be certain Vincenzo was here I would risk anything!
One thing's certain, if you don't jump you will never see that prince of yours again.
So as Stella hangs on by her finger tips she scans the faces below.

Vincenzo?

VINCENZO

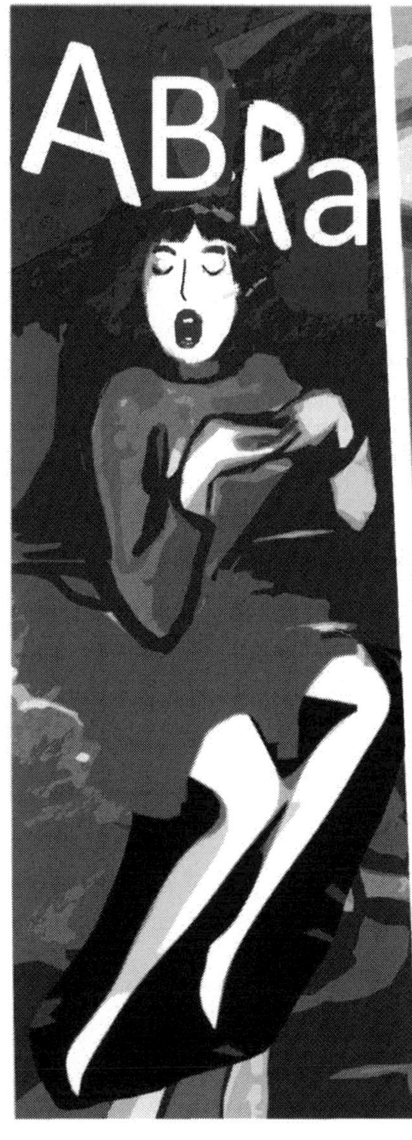
ABRa

c
ADA
BRa

Vincenzo!

***

Vincenzo!

Stella?

Stand aside lady! You are impeding the loading of this ship.
Vincenzo, it's your cross. For your safety on the voyage.

Orders are that all valuables are to be confiscated before embarcation.
It's of sentimental value only.

We don't have time for fucking sentiment. There's a war on. Or hadn't you noticed you stupid tart!

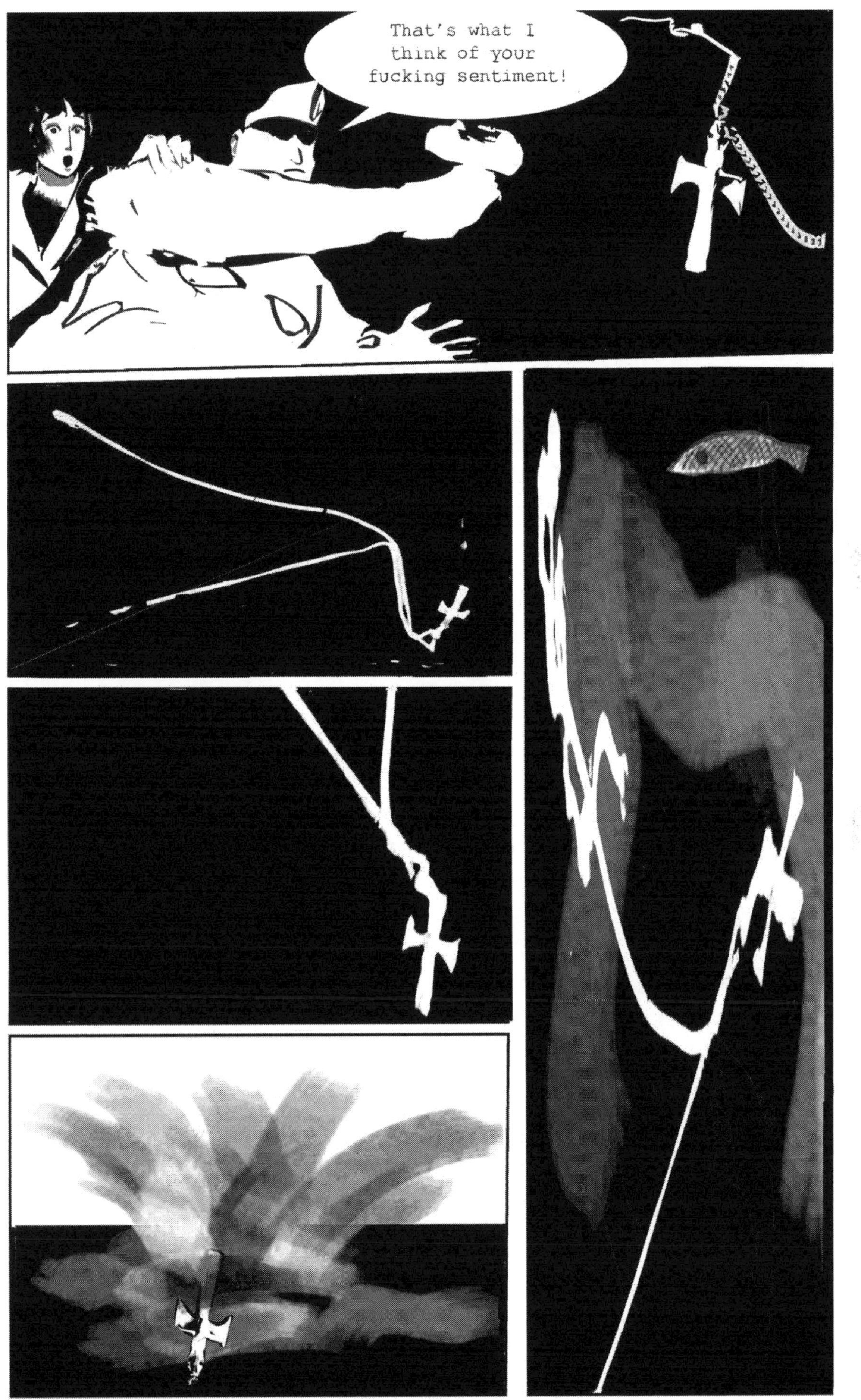
That's what I think of your fucking sentiment!

I hope the same thing happens to your greasy, wop boyfriend.

You are a disgrace to your uniform you great savage!
You'll be sacked for this. I am on a mission of national importance.

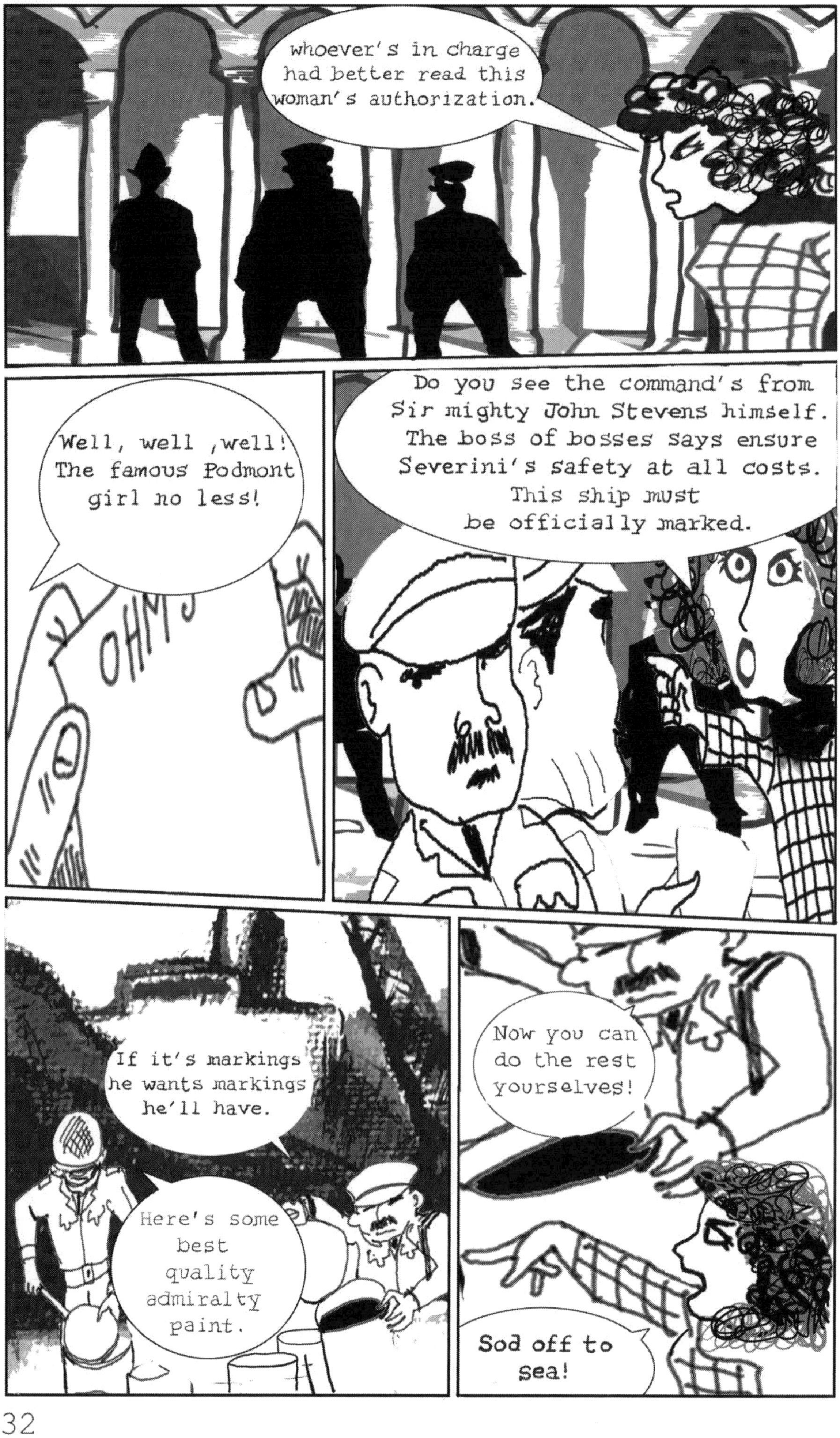

Well, well ,well! The famous Podmont girl no less!

OHMS

Do you see the command's from Sir mighty John Stevens himself. The boss of bosses says ensure Severini's safety at all costs. This ship must be officially marked.

If it's markings he wants markings he'll have.

Here's some best quality admiralty paint.

Now you can do the rest yourselves!

Sod off to sea!

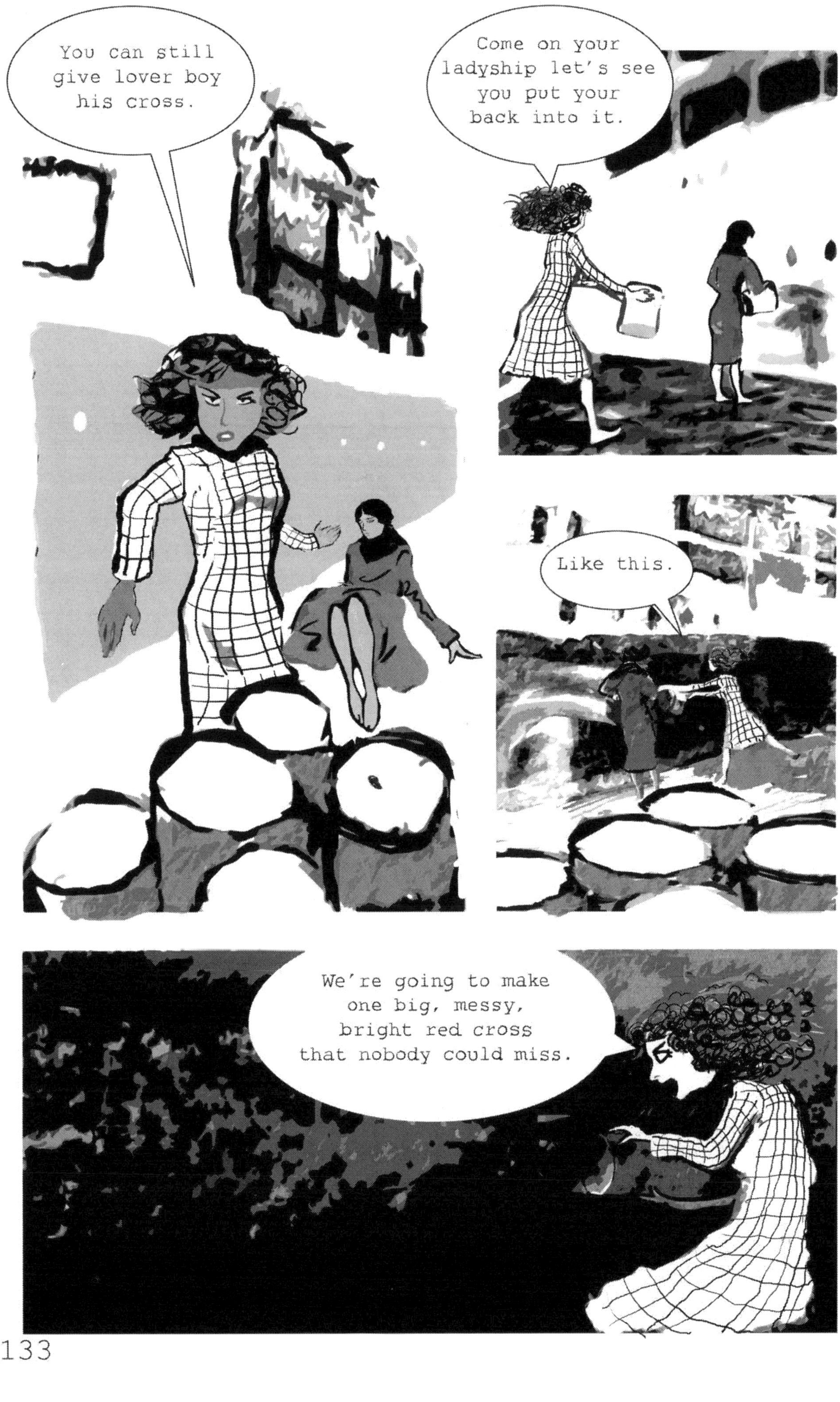

You can still give lover boy his cross.

Come on your ladyship let's see you put your back into it.

Like this.

We've just made one big red mess!

Wake up Princess! This is where we need your aristocratic sense of refinement!

I'm happier with simple gouache.
On a nice water colour pad.

Not this oily, messy old goo!
Smeared on the side of some rusty old hulk.

Let's face it, I'm just spreading the mess *around*. This is a job for experts.

who's been tampering with our bloody paint?
Same person who made that bloody mess on the side of that big tub!
I'm sure they will be reasonable once I have explained the facts.
Do you realise that you are guilty of the theft of his majesty's rust proofing solution?
To comply with your wishes would be more than my job is worth.
Just stop bollocking around and do what you're told! We are representatives of Winston Churchill and therefore of the King himself.
You've got ten minutes to paint two lines. One horizontal and one vertical.

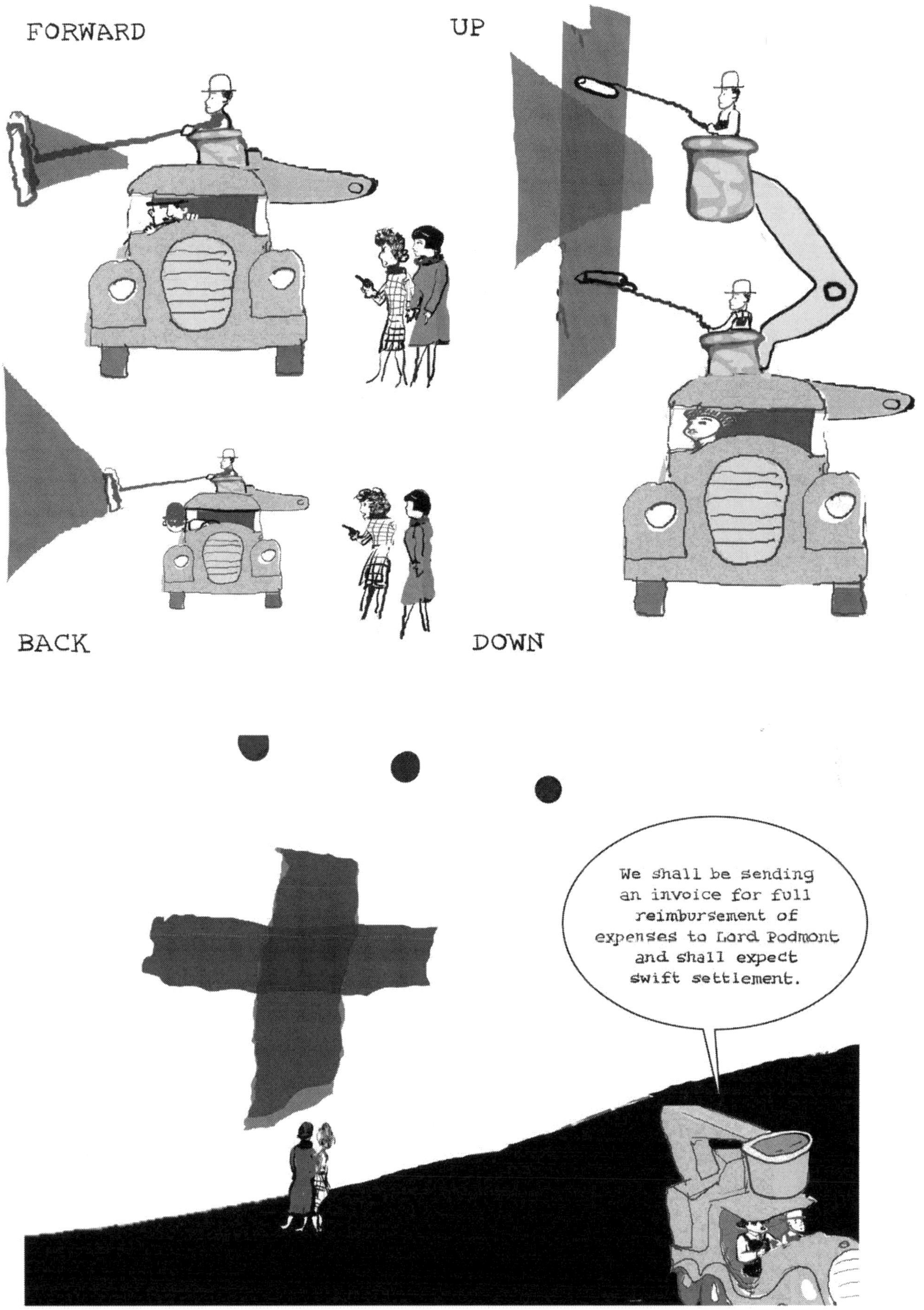

FORWARD

UP

BACK

DOWN

you could not do any more.
I could have kept my promise to keep the cross safe.

Leave it to me, Princess!

SHIT!
It's snagged.

If you want to have your cross you're going to get wet.
We'll need your delicate ladies' finishing school hands to reach it.

This isn't me!

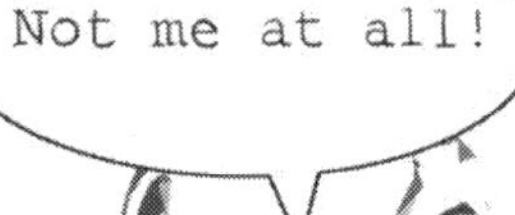
Not me at all!

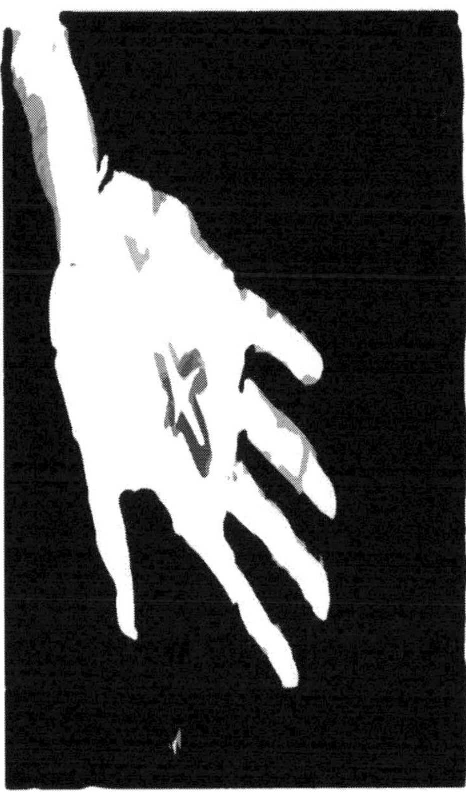

If anything
happens to
that boy of
yours I'll be
asking
questions.

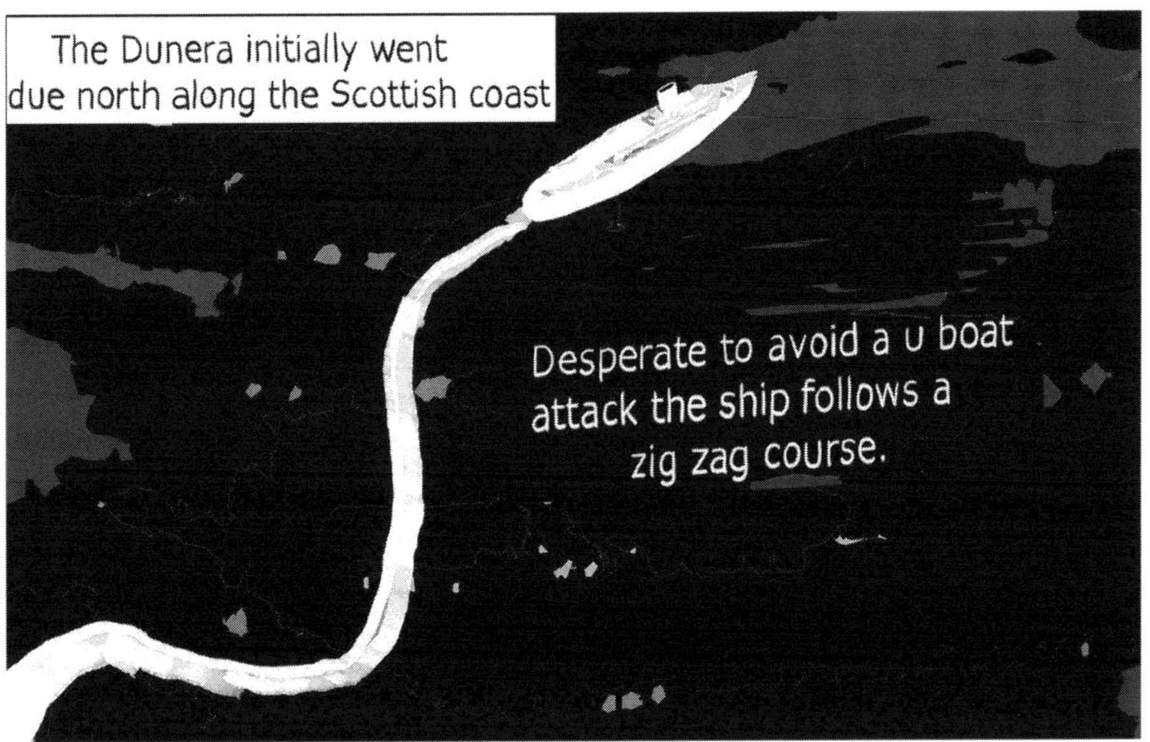
The Dunera initially went
due north along the Scottish coast
Desperate to avoid a u boat
attack the ship follows a
zig zag course.

The Italian survivors of the Arandora
are barricaded into confined quarters.

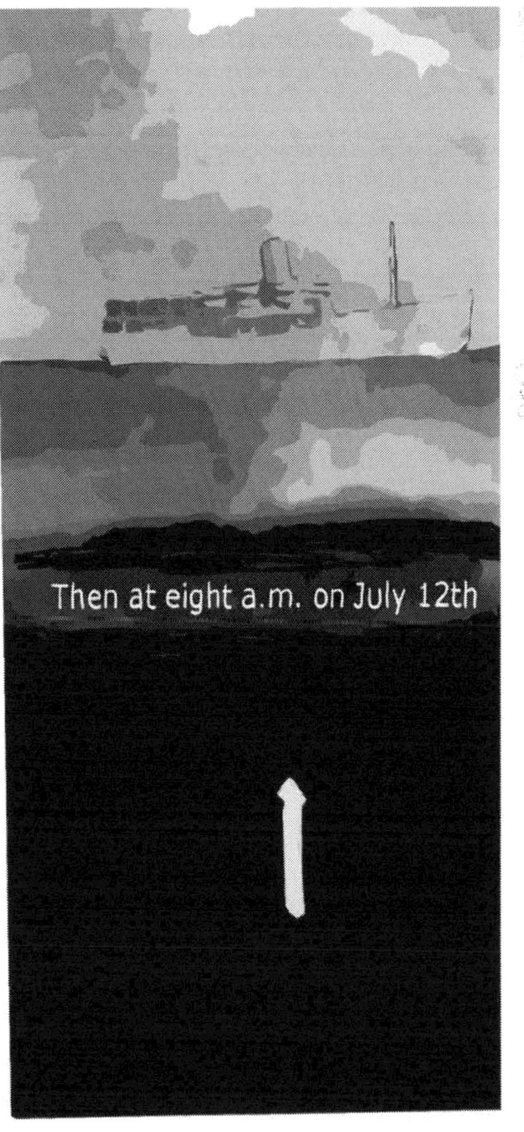
Then at eight a.m. on July 12th

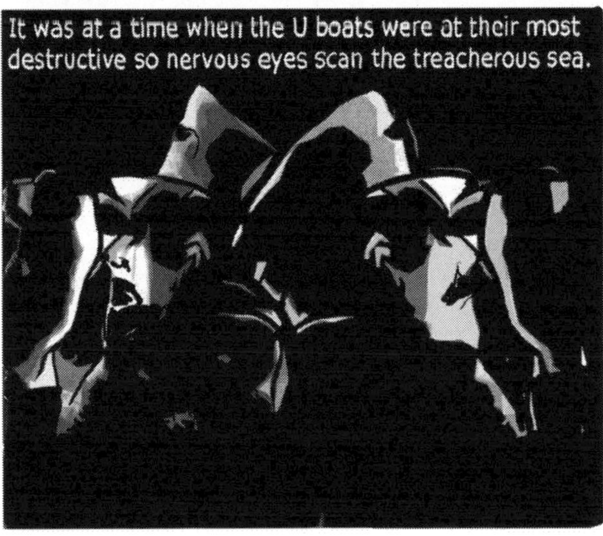
It was at a time when the U boats were at their most
destructive so nervous eyes scan the treacherous sea.

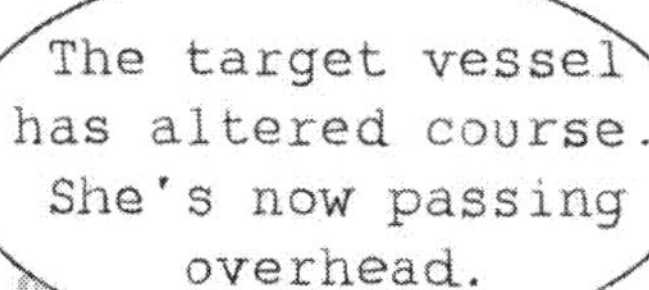
The target vessel has altered course. She's now passing overhead.

Move to attack position. Prepare torpedoes for firing.

She's a sitting duck. We can't miss.

FIRE!

BOOM
Some eye witnesses reported that the torpedo passed so close it actually bounced off the Dunera's hull before exploding close by.
Che facciamo?
No escape this time you wop scum. Drown like rats.
SLAM
Not again
MAMMA MIA
FUCKING HELL
Hard aport! Turn that wheel!

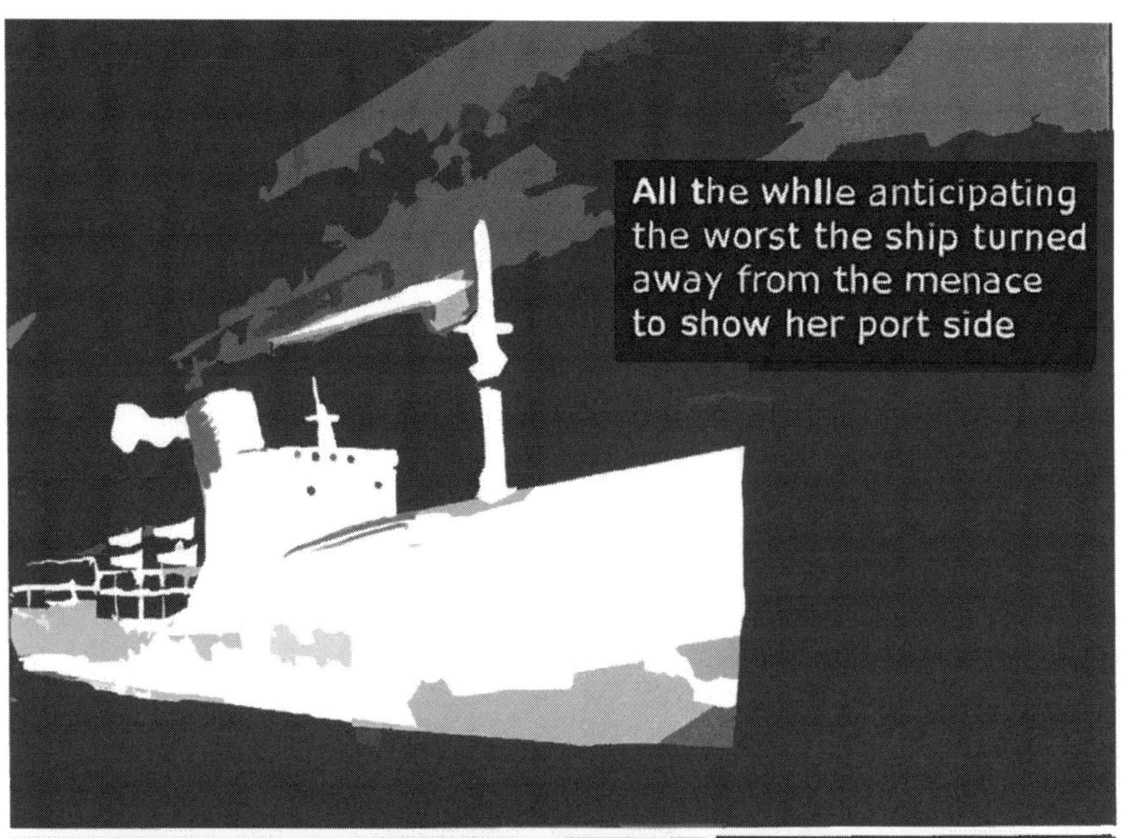
All the while anticipating
the worst the ship turned
away from the menace
to show her port side

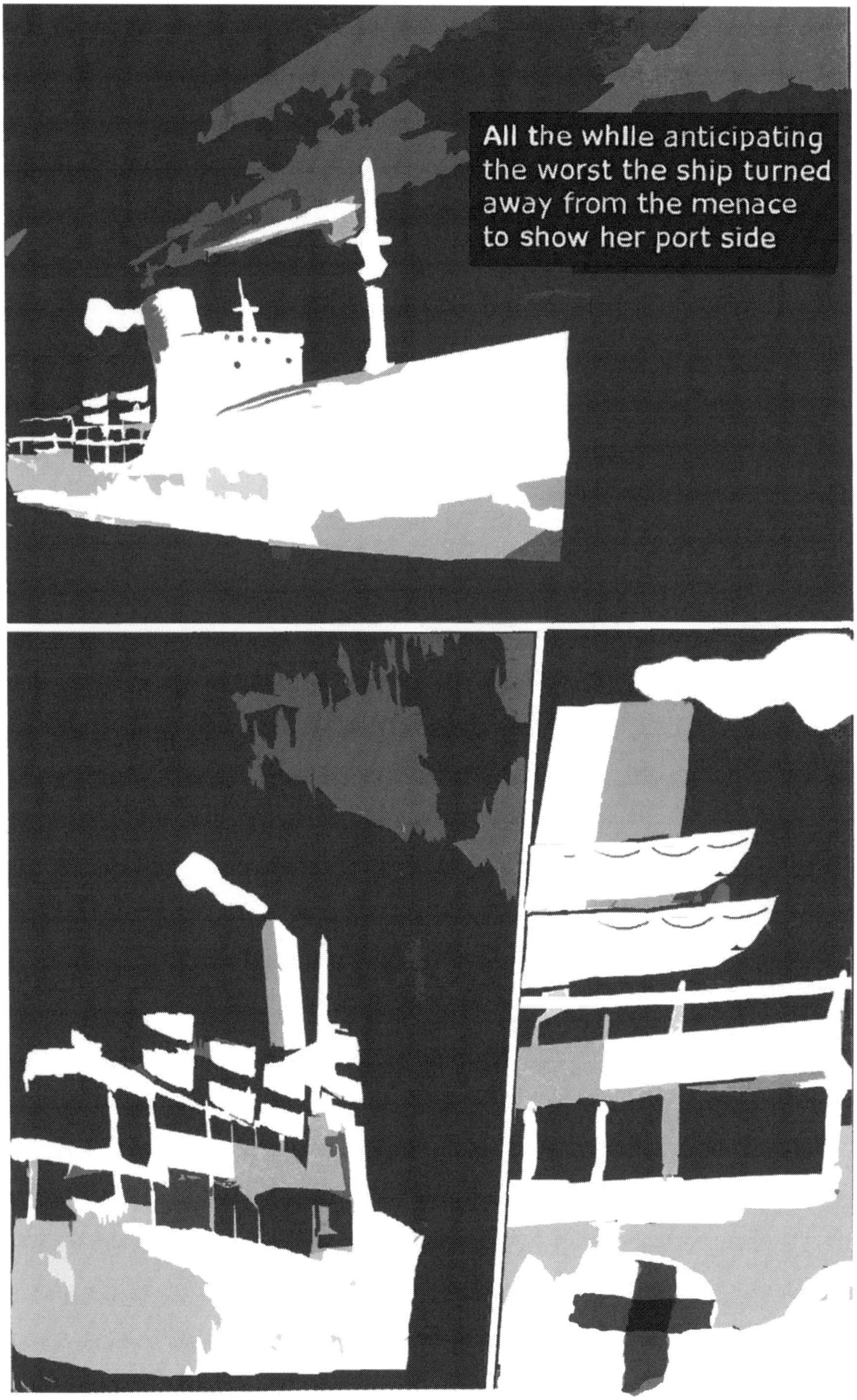

There appears to be a torpedo malfunction captain.
Ship is turning sir. She's got strange markings. Care to have a look sir?
There's something not right about that boat.
She's just too inviting.

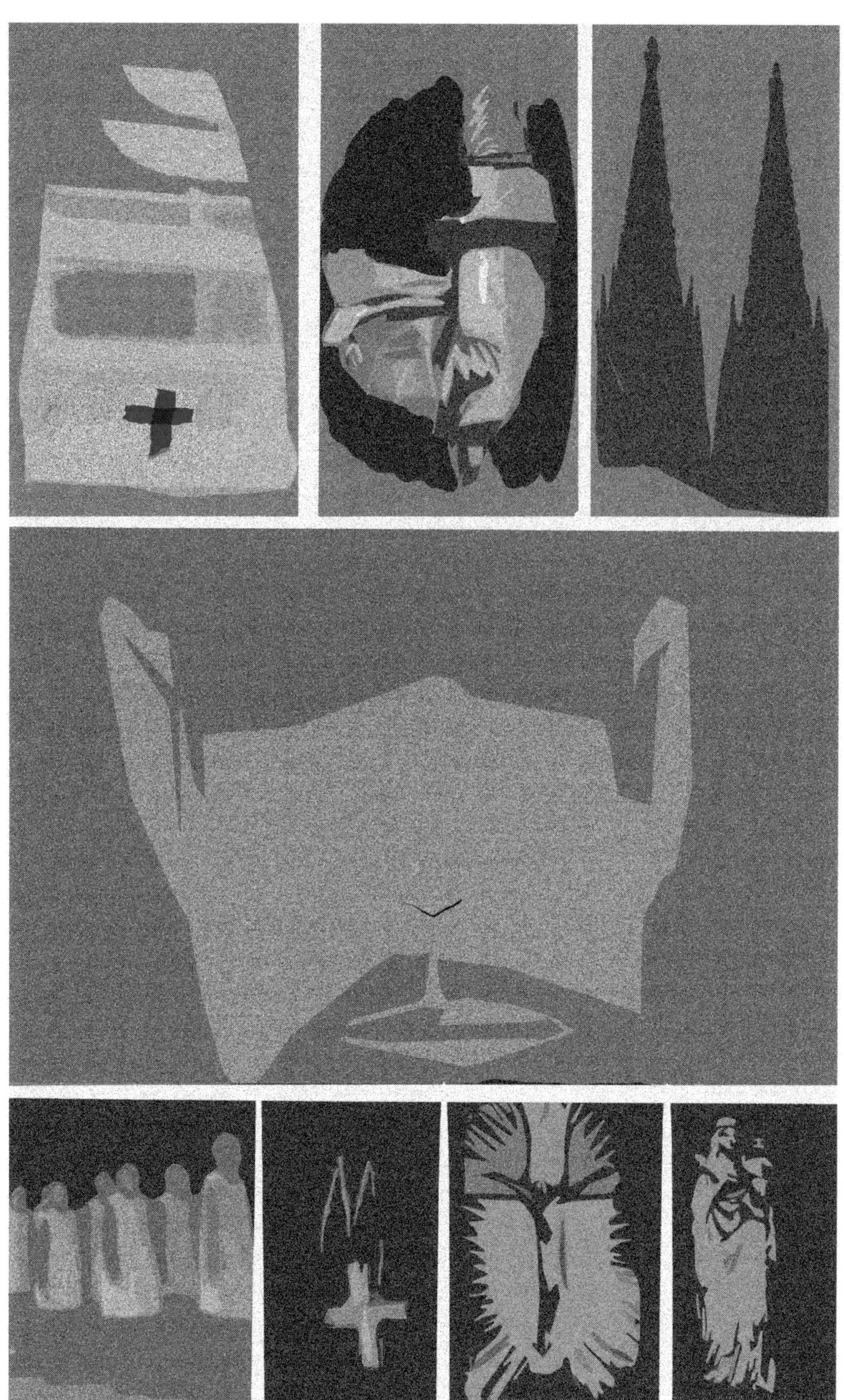

Did I ever tell you that I was once a boy chorister in Cologne Cathedral?

and so the Dunera sailed on
somewhat surprised by the
unexpected lack of attention.

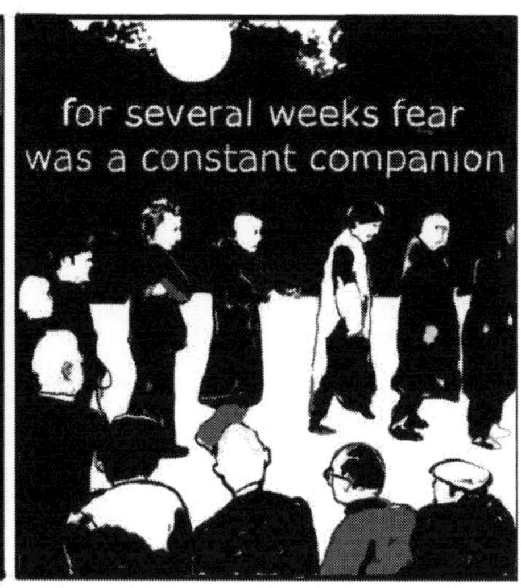
for several weeks fear
was a constant companion

As was gossip and curiosity
Madagascar?
South Africa?
Brazil?
Easter Island?

Where are we
going sonny?
I can't tell
you, you're a
war criminal!

I'm an ice-cream
maker.

Train through the outback to Tatura.

BRMMMMMMMMMM
Tatura 3 months later.

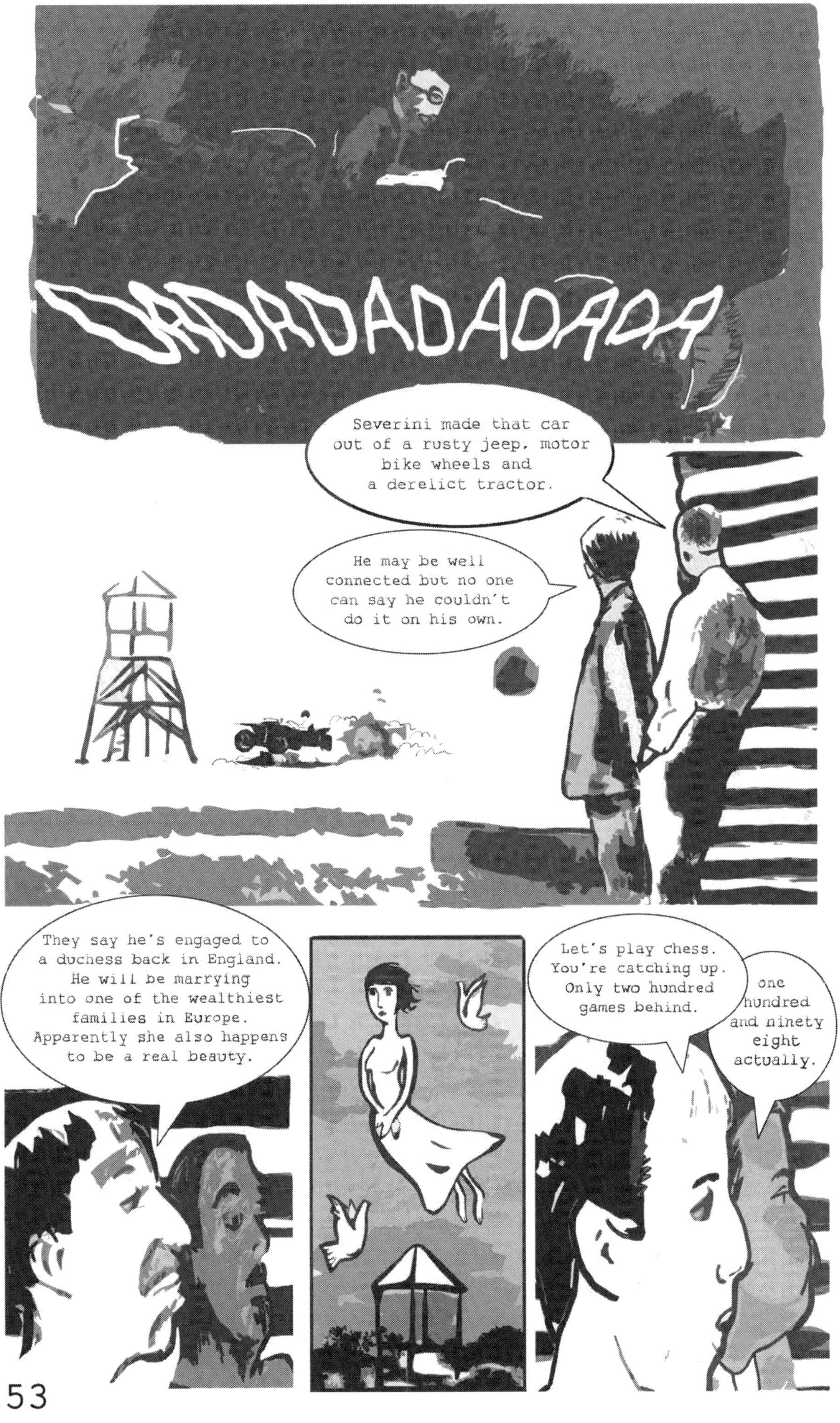

Severini made that car out of a rusty jeep, motor bike wheels and a derelict tractor.

He may be well connected but no one can say he couldn't do it on his own.

AIIIIEEEEEEEEEEE

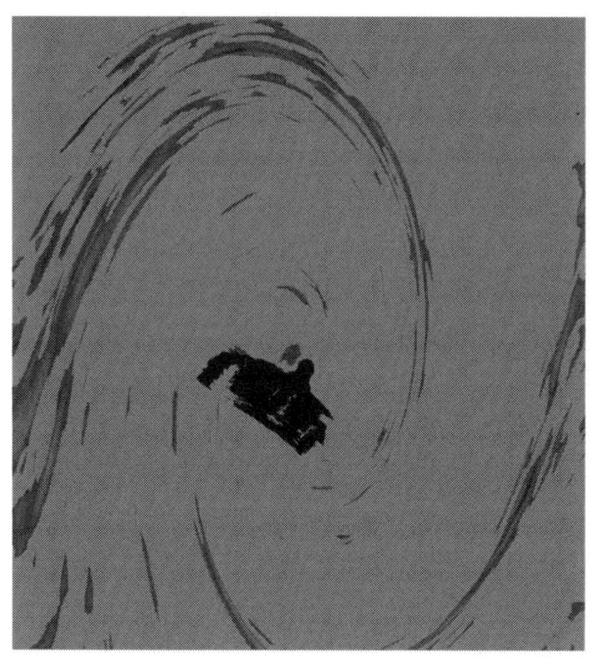

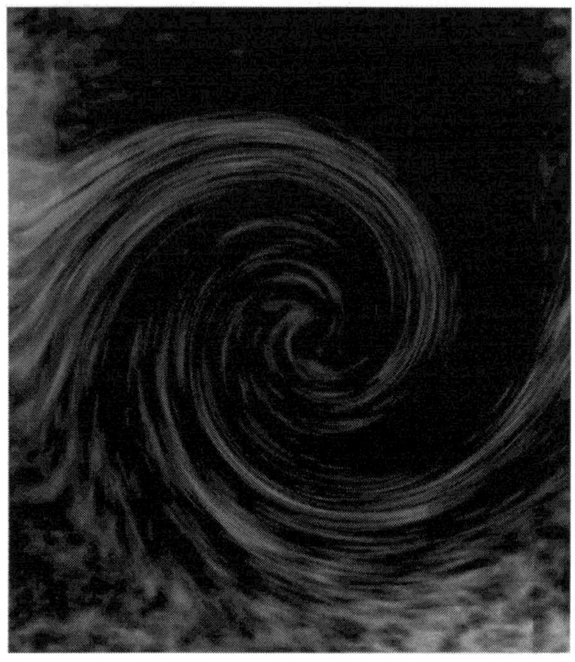

May 1941.
The Blitz had
continued for a year.
Britain stood alone in
Europe.
On the night of 11th May central
London took a mighty pounding.

Many landmark buildings
sustained terrible damage.

Westminster had its worst night.

The House of
Commons was
damaged far
beyond repair.

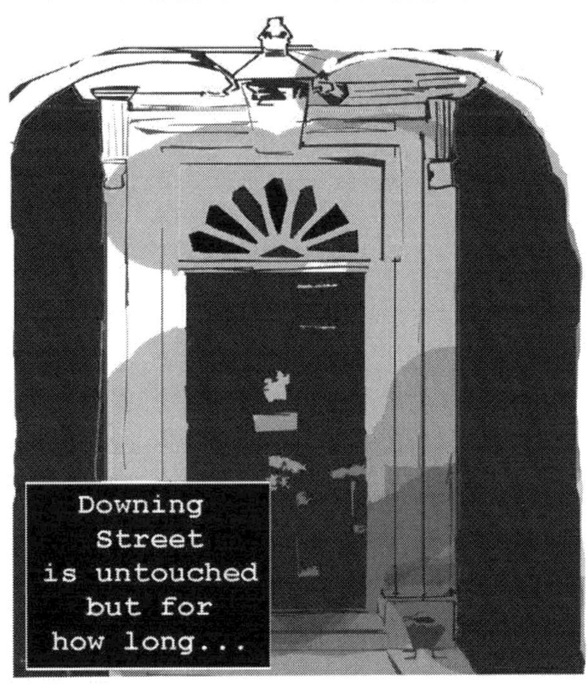
Downing
Street
is untouched
but for
how long...

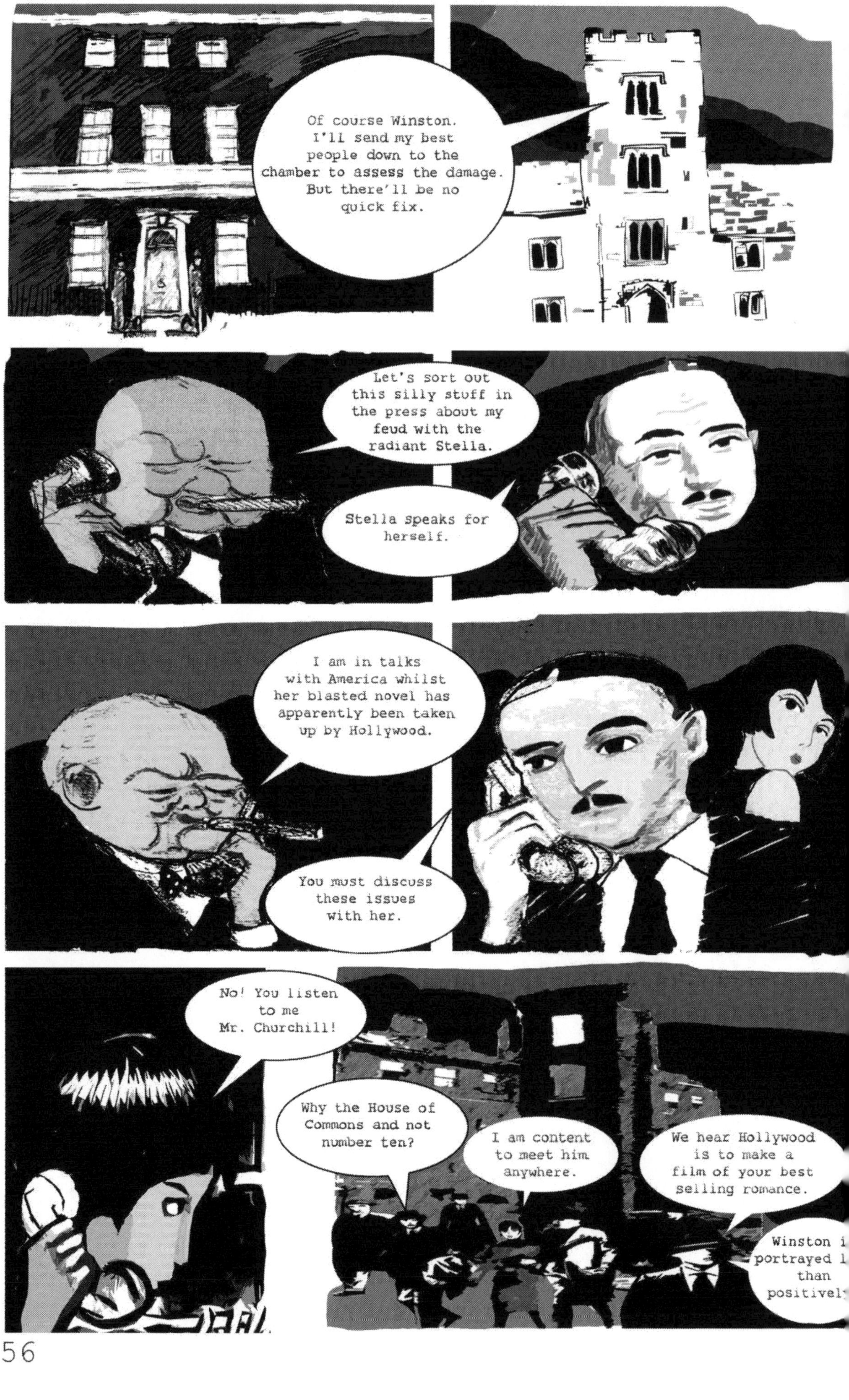

Of course Winston. I'll send my best people down to the chamber to assess the damage. But there'll be no quick fix.

Let's sort out this silly stuff in the press about my feud with the radiant Stella.

Stella speaks for herself.

I am in talks with America whilst her blasted novel has apparently been taken up by Hollywood.

You must discuss these issues with her.

Is it the time for a love story about an English woman and an enemy alien?
A coincidence that news breaks on the eve of the PM's good will trip to the US?

Stella's story, however, had captured the public's imagination.
God bless you!
Get yer lad back!

Charmed to meet you my dear.
What do you think of the Hun's antics?

We can only beat him with the support of our mighty American cousins.
One thing stops me giving unconditional support.

You need to consider how great the peril is.
This must be a most difficult day for you.
They tell me the king cried when he saw the desecration done to the abbey.

How delicate is our democracy. I am comforted by the thought of dictators riding hungry tigers who will eventually devour them.
There is a stain on your government. And you should erase it.

When I heard your American adventures were to coincide with mine I felt anger.

Your father still enjoys his freedom, privileges and huge wealth.

Some would say you're both guilty of high treason!

What is the penalty for the kidnap and murder of innocent civilians.

Good grief woman! How would it look if the empire's champion was punched on the nose by a lady novelist.

God's teeth! You're a spirited hussy. I've made generals cry with a lot less effort.
Bad though this conflict is we should remember it could get so much worse.

Our enemies are developing weapons of mass destruction.
Their rockets will atomize our defences. Storm troopers will swarm like clouds of locusts.
Moral force is only effective as support for armed force. America must enter the war soon.
Let us go to Downing Street

two hours later
The family starts with a young man falling in love with a girl.
Fine words Winston but don't forget the commission of enquiry.

two weeks later

July 1941 in the safe haven of New York City.

Lovers are reunited amidst great publicity.

Accusations of inappropriate public display collide with the need for further publicity in the cause of internees

Across the world
total war was building
to a terrible crescendo.

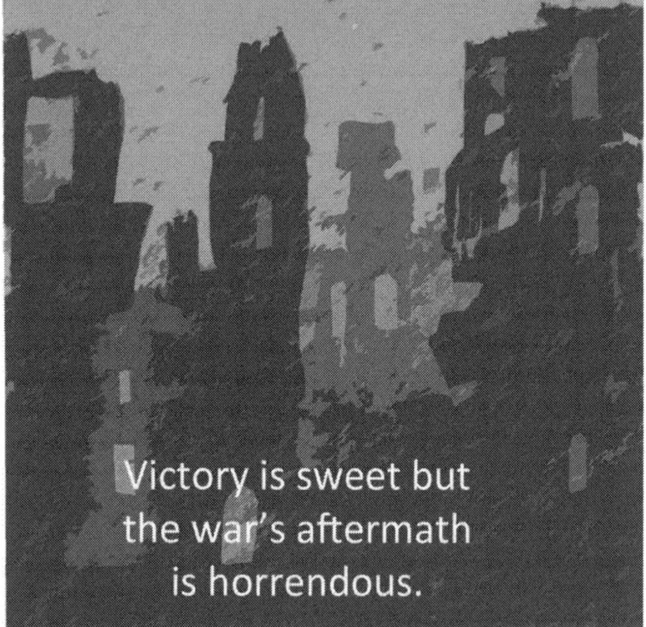

Victory is sweet but
the war's aftermath
is horrendous.

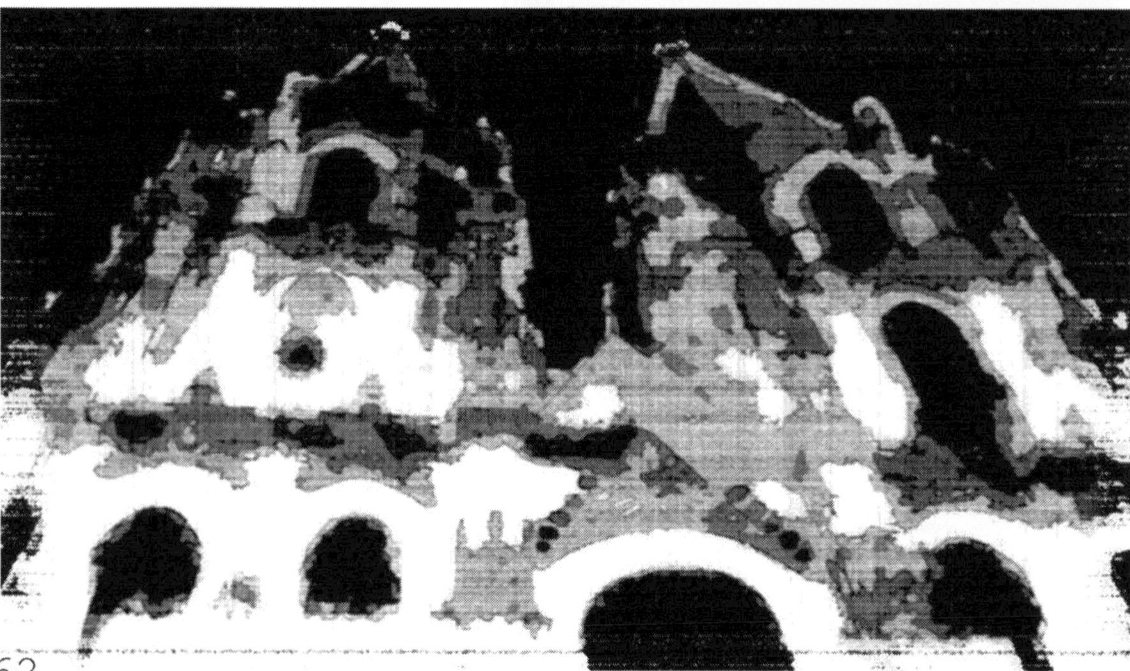

December 1945

museum of
modern art NYC

What do people see in this stuff?
Apparently this Podmont guy is a big collector.

He's a big noise in European reconstruction. The bureau is concerned about possible pinko leanings.
His glamour puss daughter and her wop husband are here to beg, borrow and even buy anti war art stuff.

Is this them now?

It's by one of those communist, European degenerates.

Men, those are salt of the earth, American patriots.

Haven't you seen the Podmont-Severini couple on all the news reels?
Didn't you see the movie based on their story?
The one where Churchill drops everything to come to their rescue.

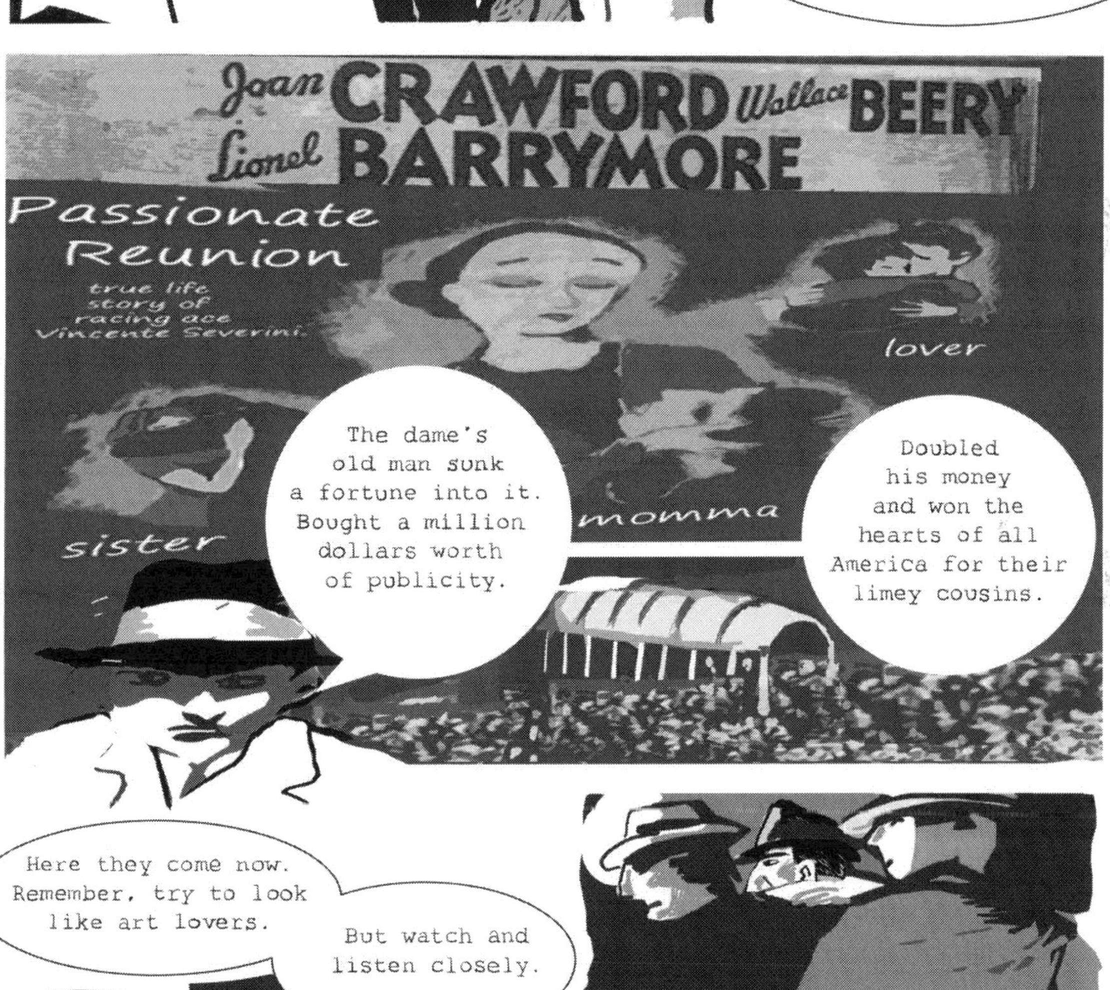

Joan CRAWFORD Wallace BEERY
Lionel BARRYMORE
Passionate Reunion
true life story of racing ace Vincente Severini.
lover
sister
momma
The dame's old man sunk a fortune into it. Bought a million dollars worth of publicity.
Doubled his money and won the hearts of all America for their limey cousins.

Here they come now. Remember, try to look like art lovers.

But watch and listen closely.

I see we
have company.

Father's art
collection is
considered a threat.
He's delighted.

They look
dangerous.
We're
famous.
It's normal.

Father's anti
war stance
has made
him unsound.

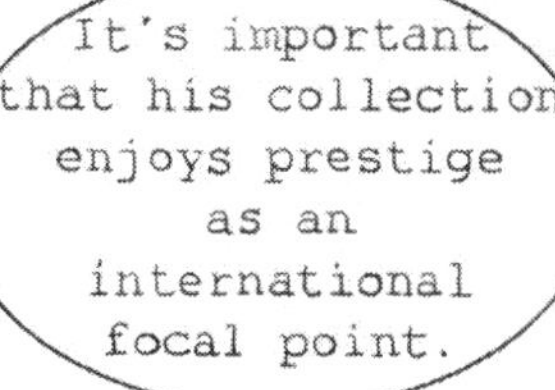
It's important
that his collection
enjoys prestige
as an
international
focal point.

He knows better
than most that
politicians will always
find ways to
justify war.

The impact of the flying bombs coupled with the destruction in Japan.
BOOM!
It was all made so very personal when that bomb struck so close to home.
He feels so protective towards your mother. It's as if he has total guilt for what happened.
It was when they stood in the middle of the bombed out shell of the estate's church that he made his promise.
He could see that desolate site's potential as a center for regenerating the spiritual universe. He was never one for small ideas.

He may be softer hearted. But he's still clear eyed.
Generous but not profligate. He makes a lot of money.

Produces the best tools for reconstruction.
All the time making a healthy profit.

He's no commie!
He's one of us!
Music to the President's ears!

His greatest fight is against those sick fascist views on art. Where any deviation from their views can be swept aside by a wave of ridicule.
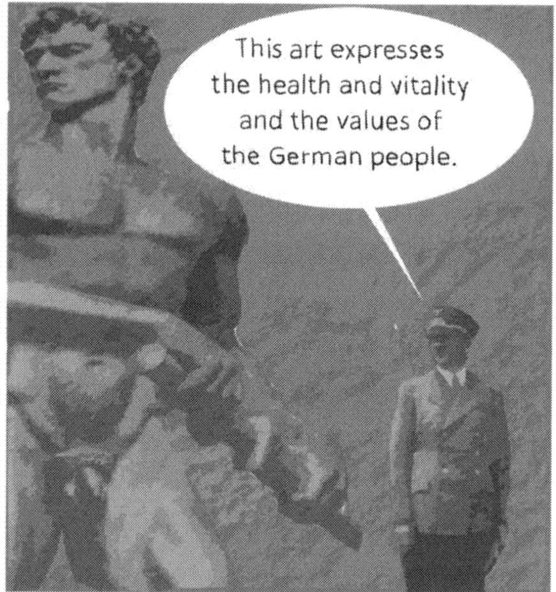
This art expresses the health and vitality and the values of the German people.

This, so called, art is Jewish, Bolshevist, Marxist and profoundly degenerate.

Here is number one on his list
Kali
Father's actions in taking a lead in the restoration will help him atone for the past.

A modern take on the Indian myth. Kali the destroyer and renewer.
I can see its significance for him.

What was thought degenerate has acquired energy.
The experimental and abstract are most admired.

State support of artists demands artists support the state. No ifs, no buts.
There speaks the shadow minister for the arts.

Should have quietly rebuilt it
It's a bloody ruin!
It's a symbol.

Bloody steps!
The King loves it.
The king had better not take a tumble.

Smacks of arrogance filling a lovely old medieval church with transient lefty trash.
Father, you haven't seen anything yet.

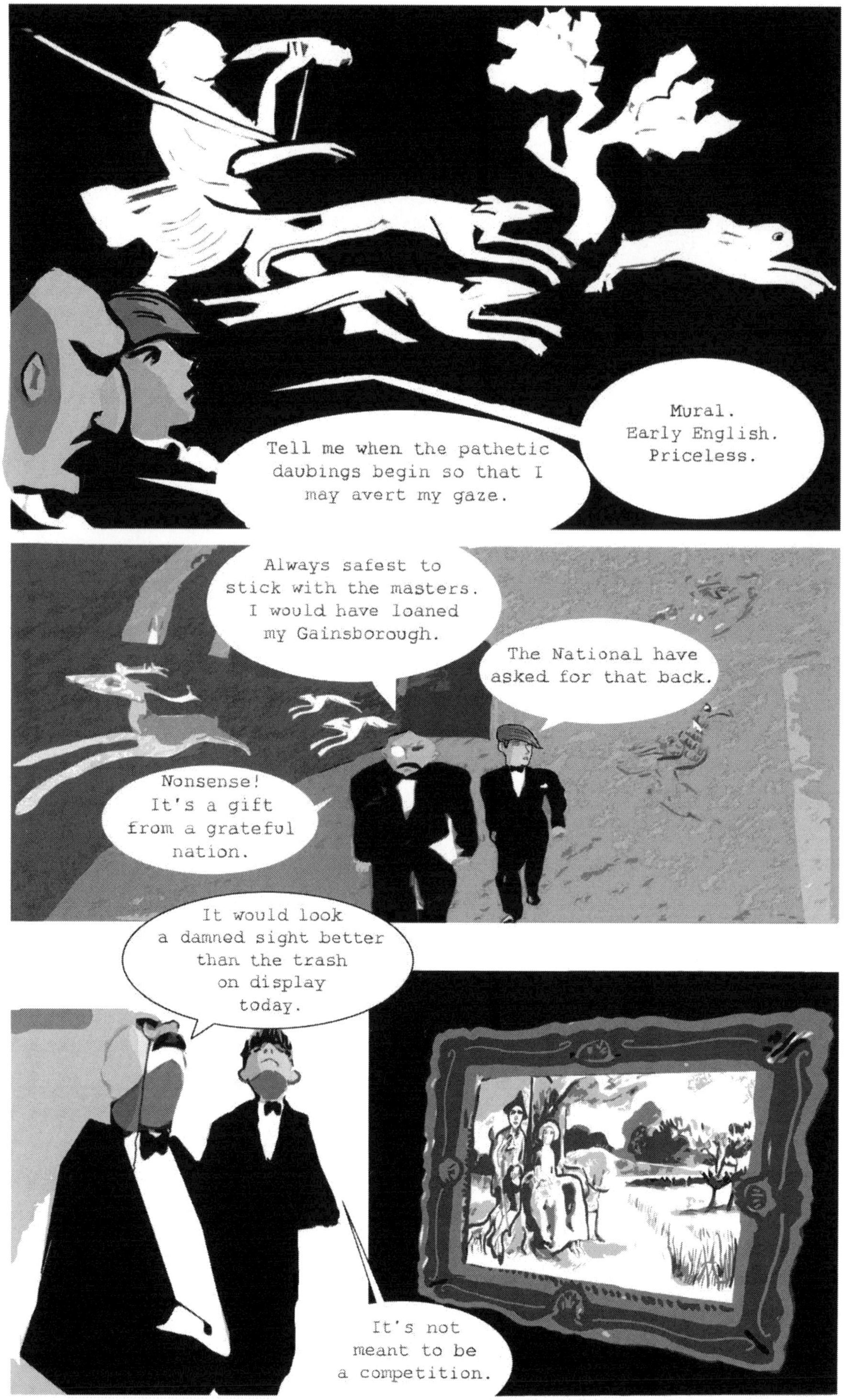

Always safest to stick with the masters. I would have loaned my Gainsborough.

The National have asked for that back.

Nonsense! It's a gift from a grateful nation.

It would look a damned sight better than the trash on display today.

It's not meant to be a competition.

INFANTILE! DECADENT! RUBBISH!

That's exactly what Hitler would have said.
AND?

German abstract. Lucky it wasn't destroyed by the Nazis.
Lucky for whom?

What possible criteria were applied to the collection of such trash?
The absolute qualification for inclusion is that each artist was branded degenerate by the Nazis.
Garbage!
Blasphemy!
Excrement!
Vile!
This exhibition will be the focus for artistic debate for generations to come.
Hurry along gentlemen. The king is about to speak.

I require an urgent word in your shell-like Podmont, old man.

If you want to cling to your dubious career you would do well to listen.

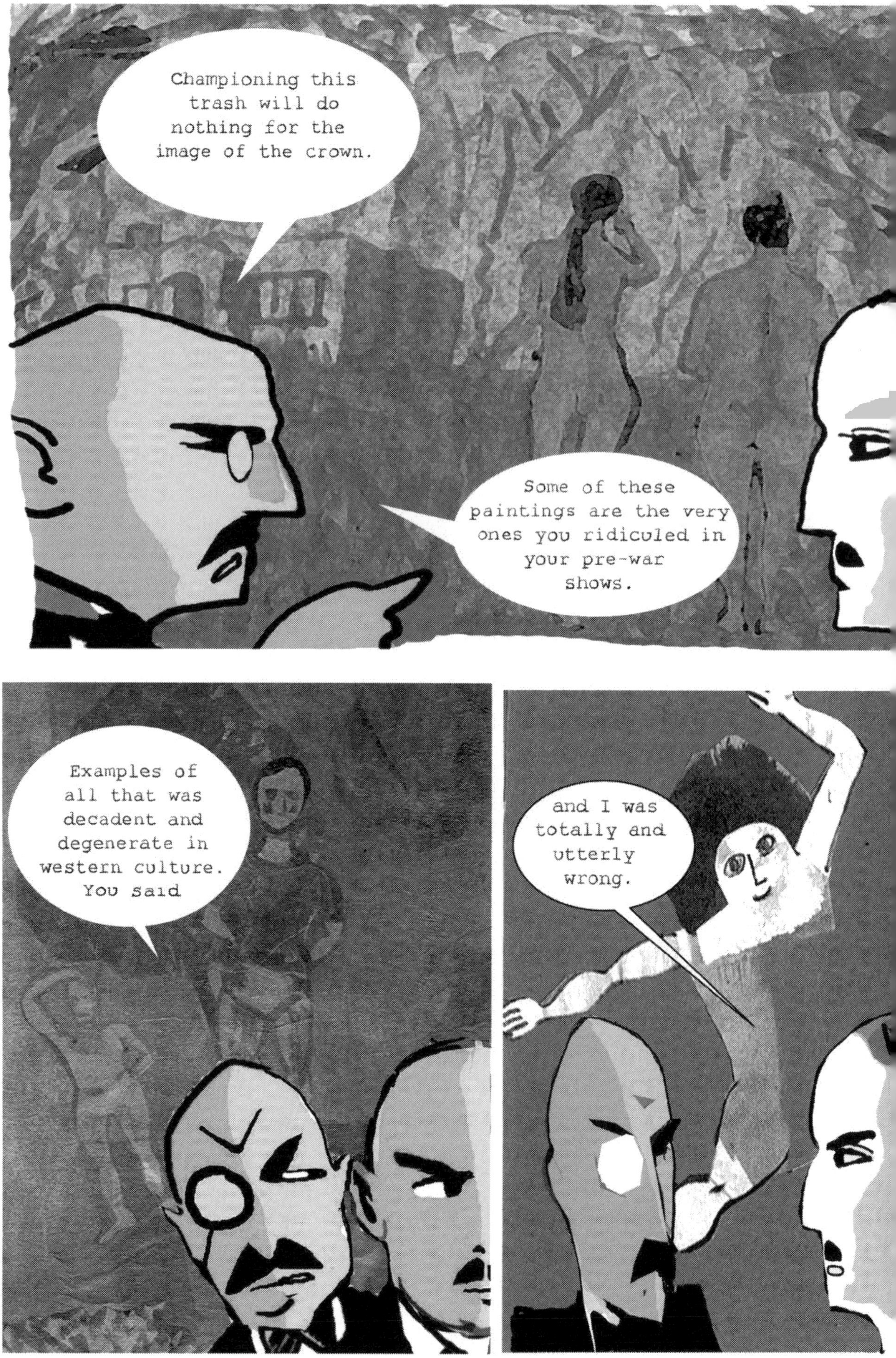

Championing this trash will do nothing for the image of the crown.

Some of these paintings are the very ones you ridiculed in your pre-war shows.

two hours later

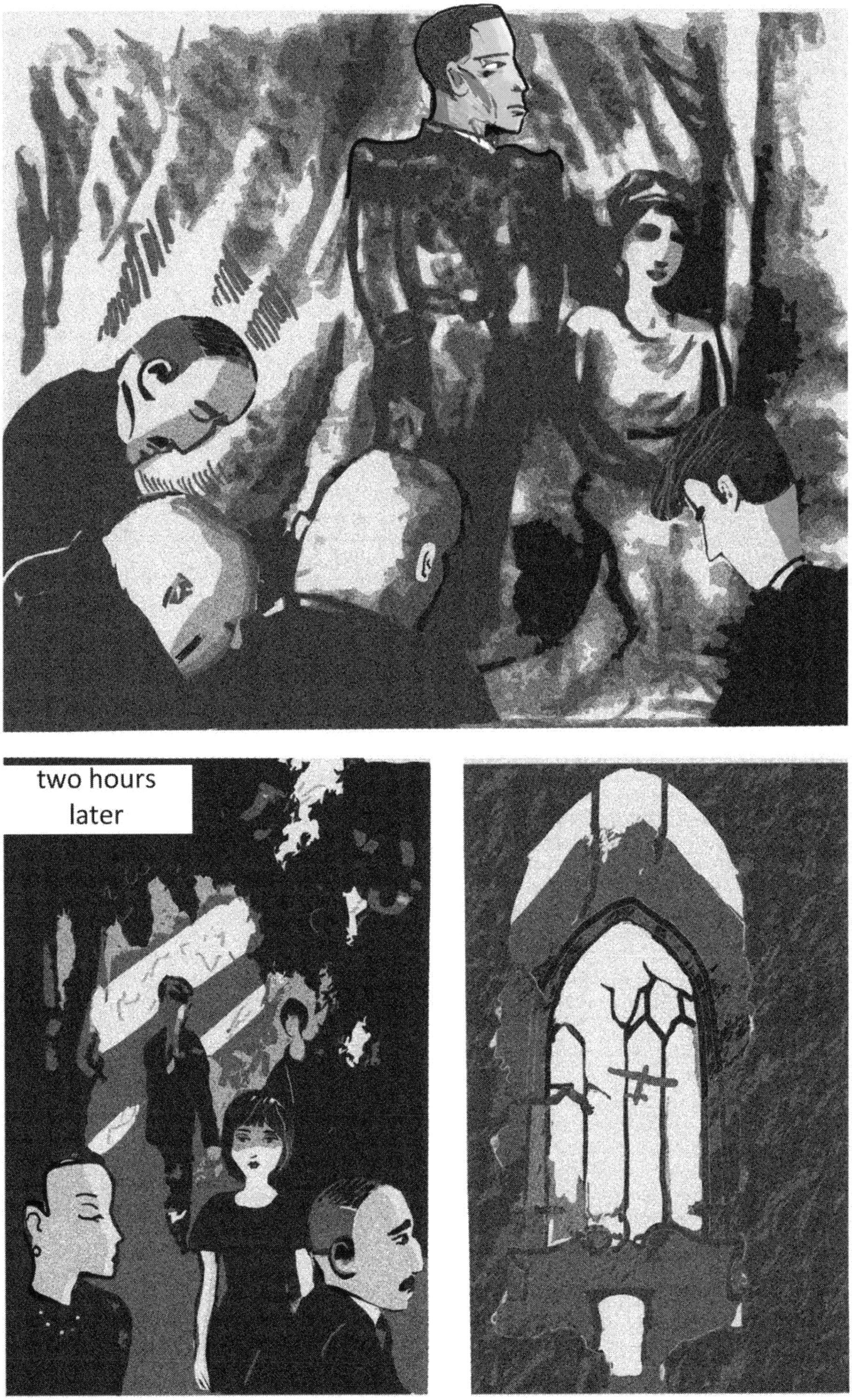

Maria it's understandable that you should want a private view.

The collection is drawn from artists suppressed by the fascist regimes.

These images capture and convey the pain and madness of war.

And, Maria, remember that the focus of the whole exhibition will be on the fate of the Arandora Star.

The state of the unrestored walls of this ancient church and its rescued treasures will remind us of the mindless vandalism of war.

Memorials will allow people to reflect on more local and personal tragedy.

And then to climb the staircase up towards the light.

To finish with the particular tragedy strongly associated with this very place and two of the families that have been so affected by it.

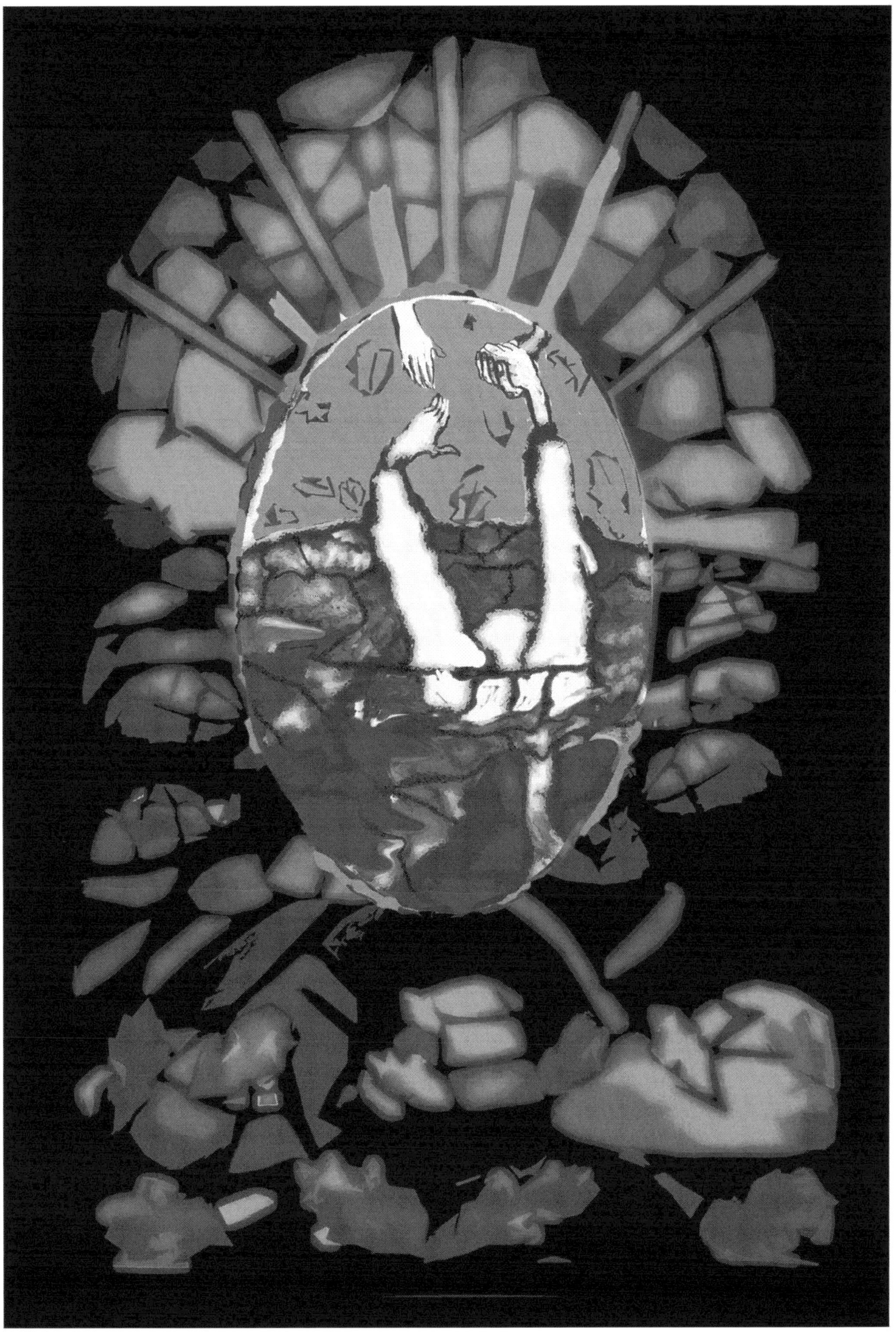

Thankyou.

Whilst remembering the dead it also pays tribute to those who, like Stella, would save life.

What's your response Vincenzo?

I think that it is a delightful piece of art that will bring comfort to many..

But for Antonio..

We revive the Podmont racing team and we build the world's fastest racing car.

You know all efforts have been diverted to the huge task of European reconstruction and recovery.

And now is the time to reconstruct Antonio's life's work and build a world beating car.
Father, we need to get you out of crypts. You're turning into Count Dracula.
When did you last have a good night's sleep?
First we reconstruct the car and then we reconstruct the world's greatest road race!
Mille Miglia!
I drive you navigate.
What a lovely idea!

Podmont!
Wake up man!

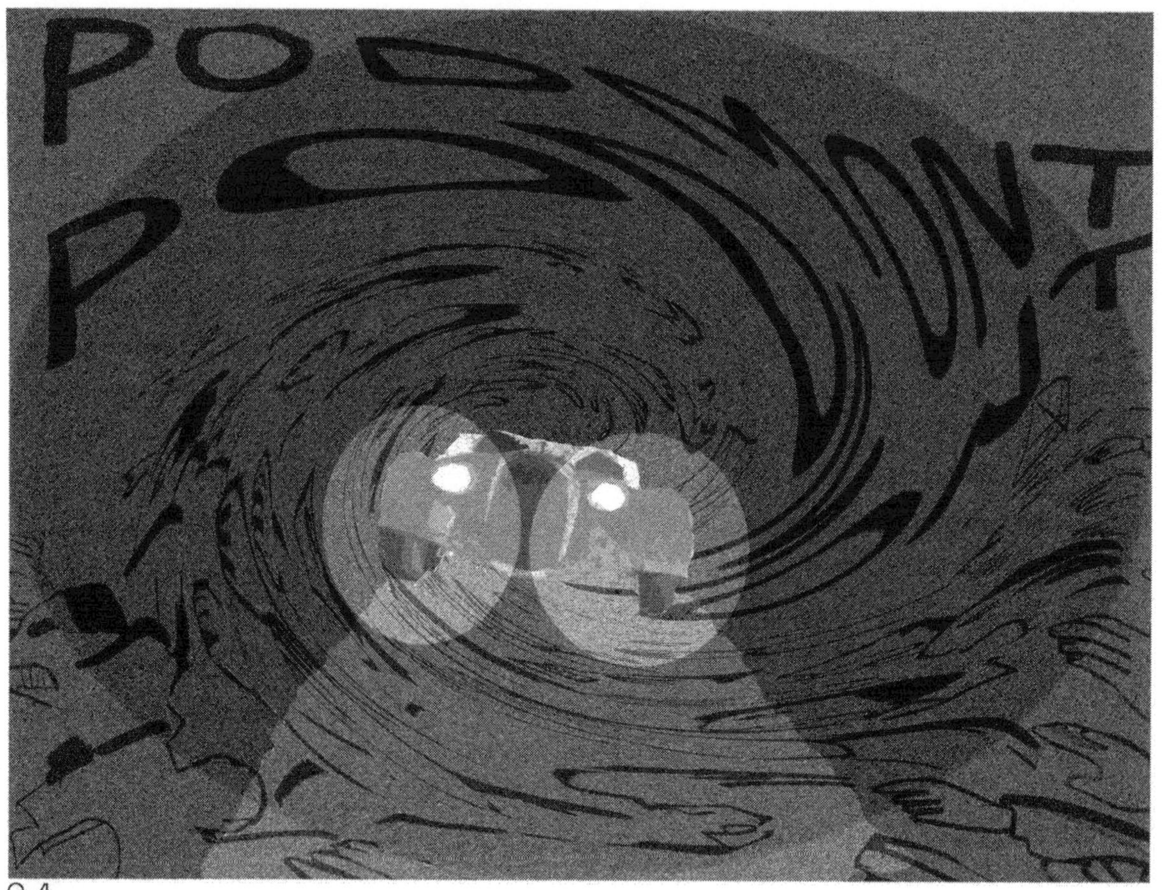

Open your eyes man and concentrate on those bends!

Just one car in front.

We're going to win this beautiful race!
Two miles to go!

hairpin next.
First gear.
BRMMMMMMM

hard down!
MMMMMMMMMMMMMMM

We can still win if
you can concentrate!
Same to you!
incline for two
hundred metres.

You've perked up
Podmont!

ROARRRRRRRRRRRRR
We've got the lead!
ROARRRRRRRRRRRRRRR

Sun's out!

Final bend!

Ascending straight to
the finish line.

YOU'VE GOT US HOME PODMONT!
WITH A LITTLE HELP!

PODMONT, IT'S OVER!

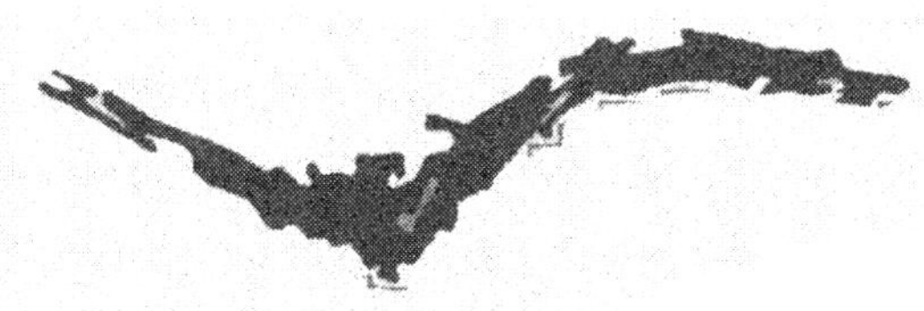

The End

POSTSCRIPT

as for Winston Churchill....

How could anything match those glory years.

Thoughts turned to posterity.

The image produced was not always wholly satisfactory.

Such images, no matter how well intentioned, could not be allowed to endure. Winston must take his place in the pantheon of heroes.

The Wildwoman had her wish and her cameo in the Podmont Production lead to increasing prominence until she had achieved the star status she craved.
TITANIA
A MIDSUMMER NIGHT'S DREAM
A MIDSUMMER NIGHT'S DREAM
TITANIA
TARZAN AND HIS MATE
TARZAN AND HIS MATE
WILDWOMAN AND HER MATE

PODMONT

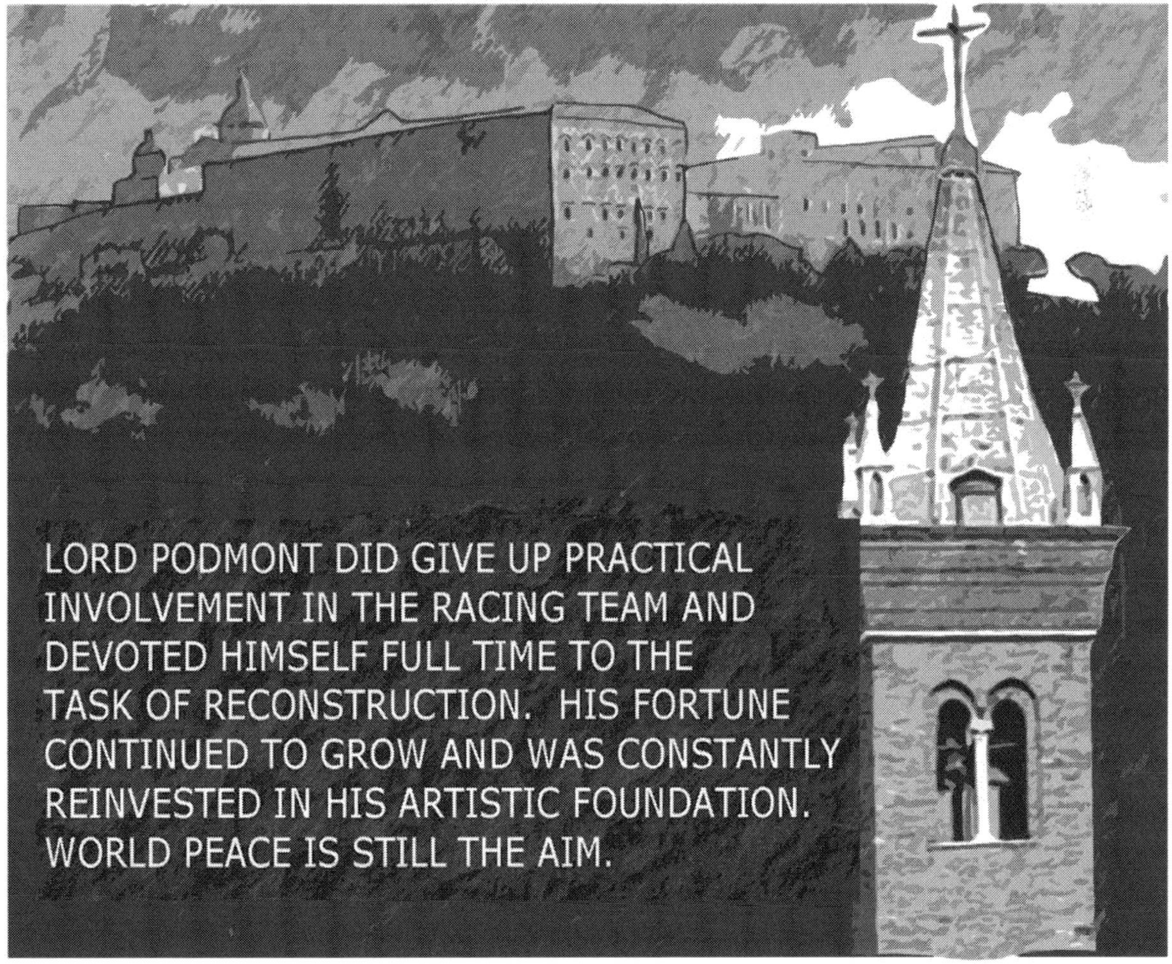
LORD PODMONT DID GIVE UP PRACTICAL
INVOLVEMENT IN THE RACING TEAM AND
DEVOTED HIMSELF FULL TIME TO THE
TASK OF RECONSTRUCTION. HIS FORTUNE
CONTINUED TO GROW AND WAS CONSTANTLY
REINVESTED IN HIS ARTISTIC FOUNDATION.
WORLD PEACE IS STILL THE AIM.

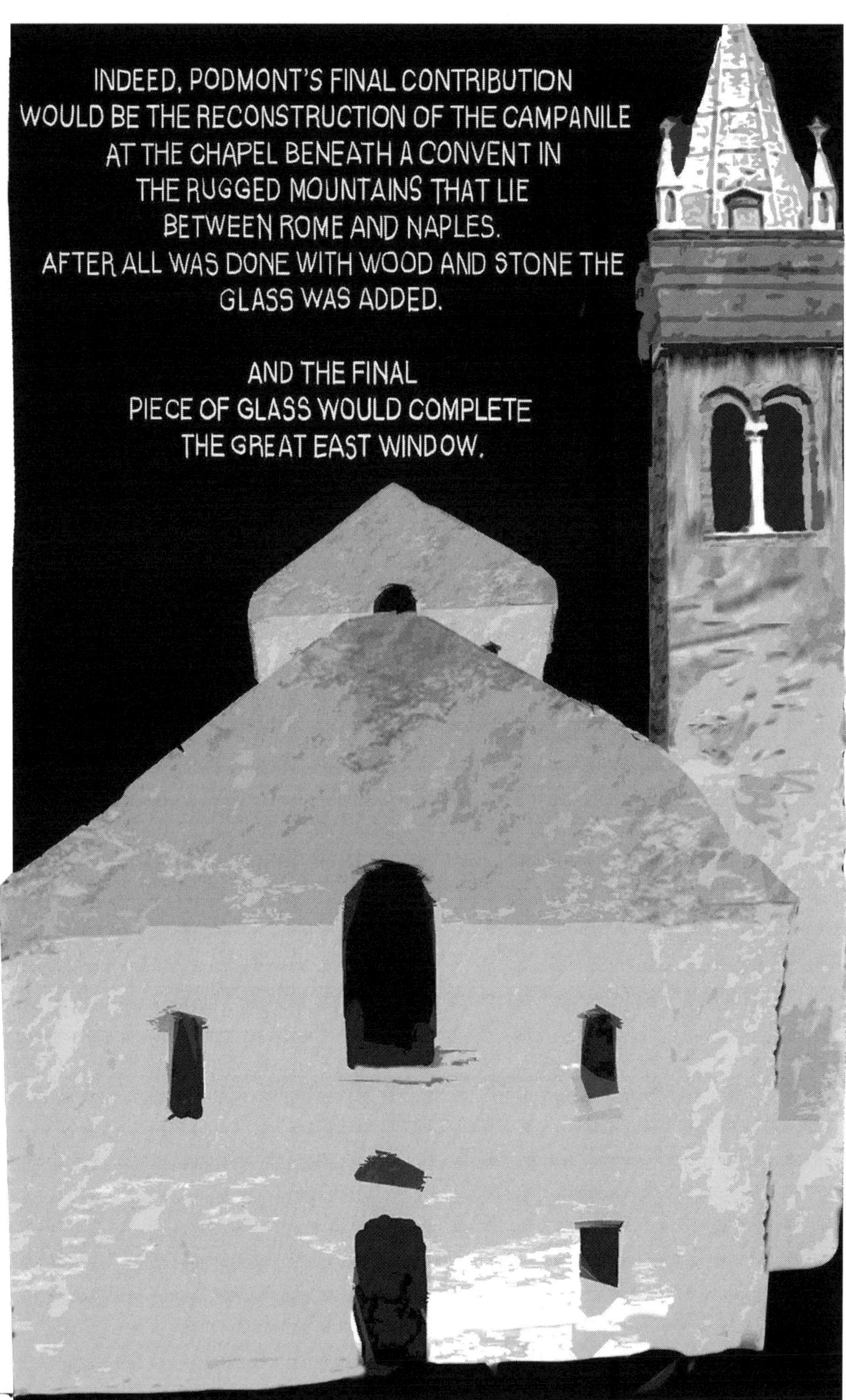
INDEED, PODMONT'S FINAL CONTRIBUTION
WOULD BE THE RECONSTRUCTION OF THE CAMPANILE
AT THE CHAPEL BENEATH A CONVENT IN
THE RUGGED MOUNTAINS THAT LIE
BETWEEN ROME AND NAPLES.
AFTER ALL WAS DONE WITH WOOD AND STONE THE
GLASS WAS ADDED.
AND THE FINAL
PIECE OF GLASS WOULD COMPLETE
THE GREAT EAST WINDOW.

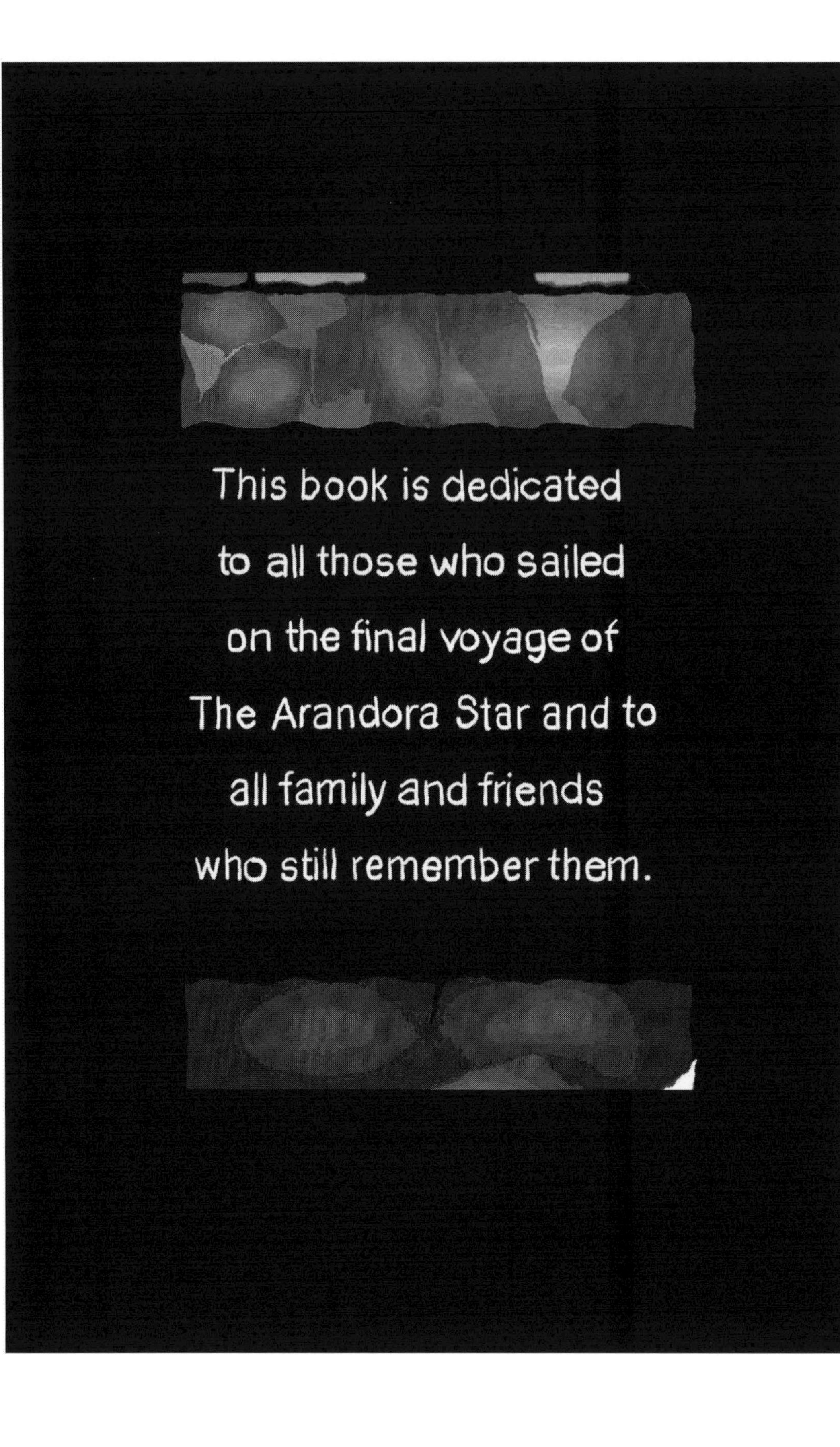
This book is dedicated
to all those who sailed
on the final voyage of
The Arandora Star and to
all family and friends
who still remember them.

12128375R00116

Printed in Great Britain
by Amazon